Rebound

Rebound

SPORTS, COMMUNITY,
AND THE
INCLUSIVE CITY

Perry King

COACH HOUSE BOOKS, TORONTO

first edition

Published with the generous assistance of the Canada Council for the Arts and the Ontario Arts Council. Coach House Books also acknowledges the support of the Government of Canada through the Canada Book Fund and the Government of Ontario through the Ontario Book Publishing Tax Credit.

LIBRARY AND ARCHIVES CANADA CATALOGUING IN PUBLICATION

Title: Rebound : sports, community, and the inclusive city / Perry King.
Names: King, Perry (Journalist), author.
Identifiers: Canadiana (print) 20210299959 | Canadiana (ebook) 20210300000 | ISBN 9781552454251 (softcover) | ISBN 9781770566743 (EPUB) | ISBN 9781770566750 (PDF)
Subjects: LCSH: Sports—Social aspects. | LCSH: City and town life. | LCSH: Community life. | LCSH: Social participation.
Classification: LCC GV706.5 .K56 2021 | DDC 306.4/83—dc23

Rebound is available as an ebook: ISBN 978 1 77056 674 3 (EPUB), ISBN 978 1 77056 675 0 (PDF)

To Andrew,
For planting the seeds of this project

To Hilary,
For helping those seeds grow

TABLE OF CONTENTS

I
WHY DO SPORTS EVEN MATTER?

M asaryk-Cowan is one of the best places not on a main street. Tucked away from Queen Street West in south Parkdale, Masaryk-Cowan Community Recreation Centre has been a constant in my life for a long time. I was sent to daycare there. I learned to play pool there and attended a bunch of community events with my mom. It was a place of refuge when I wasn't ready to go home and study after school.

It still stands today, not all that different from my childhood, always bustling with kids and parents alike. The interior exposed brick on some of the centre's walls awed me as a kid – I lived in an apartment building, so go figure.

Named in honour of Tomáš Masaryk, Czechoslovakia's first president, this old building has been a Parkdale social fixture for decades. The south portion of the building was built in 1898 and housed a curling club. In 1907, it was an indoor roller-skating rink. In 1915 it became the Pavlova Dancing Academy, a popular dance hall. In the thirties and forties, the academy evolved into a tennis club and a rec centre for wartime employees. Today, the building itself is heritage designated.

The centre is a place that I grew to admire because it was where people from the neighbourhood could expand their horizons. Friends of mine practised karate there, earning black belts. The upstairs community rooms once held a radio station – they probably still do, actually.

Then there's the basketball court. For years, that court was the site of numerous late Tuesday and Friday night pickup games. I would meet kids and teens who lived in the neighbourhood –

they went to Parkdale Junior and Senior Public School and Queen Victoria Public School, and a lot of the older kids went to Parkdale Collegiate. (I attended a Catholic school and didn't socialize with them otherwise.) Many of them needed a place to go. How did I know? Because I needed a place to go, too. I was too young to get a job and too old to be hanging around the house. And on that ball court, with its slippery hardwood, its fluorescent lighting, and that glass-panelled ceiling, I found a place to move, to get the angry and nervous energy out.

That court, and every game there, was lively. People cared about winning, if only as a moral or personal victory. Everyone was so athletic, so cerebral. You called your own fouls, you argued on your team's behalf – and, in some cases, players took three-point shots to settle call disputes. (Side note: I feel that three-point shots to settle court disputes should be a thing in the pros. But that's for another conversation.) There may have been an elbow, maybe a fist. Nothing ever escalated into anything too personal for me. There were no 'Do you want to take this outside?' moments. If you weren't playing, you were hanging around the stage, which hosted community theatre from time to time, or the elevated walking areas that abutted the court on the sides. You got up there via the stairs on each side, and the view down to the court – heck, the view of the entire community centre – was amazing. But it was the game, and the culture, that bustled on the court below.

Masaryk's court gave me a lot of joy, but also one of my first glimpses into the world of sports. If I'm being quite honest, it was the place that provided one of the first moments that inspired my writing career – a real eye-opener as to what sport can represent in people's lives.

I was twenty-one years old at the time, and still wondering whether sports writing would be my path. Freshly graduated, underemployed, and still living with my mother, I hadn't yet decided to go back to school to study journalism. There were many questions swimming in my head: Was I going to get the job I wanted? Was I doing enough to develop my skills and experience in the field? Yet there was little doubt about what I intended to do, and I didn't care how long it took to get there: I wanted to write about sports.

But I didn't know what kind of writer I wanted to be, what kind of voice to evoke, and where I wanted to put my focus. What mattered? What stories needed to be told? What sports did I care about? For that matter, why do sports even matter? Who cares about sports, anyway?

• • •

Masaryk-Cowan, and the people who walked through it and lived in it, were a litmus test, the true barometer of the neighbourhood's character. Parkdale, as my wife describes it sometimes, is an 'honest' neighbourhood – a place that shows itself for what it really is, in its local businesses, its places to convene, the things that happen there, and, especially, in its people. The Statistics Canada census data provides only a small glimpse: Parkdale, with over 108,000 residents as of 2019, is a village of different languages, religions, and cultures, all packed into about fourteen square kilometres! And dense. Indeed, when I walk around Queen Street West at any time of day, it's almost always crowded with people.

I have always seen Parkdale's changing faces and places as a reflection of the world at large. I grew up there in the 1980s, 1990s, and 2000s, when a lot of immigrants came to Canada to escape political turmoil in their home countries or in search of new opportunities for themselves and their families. Those identities were reflected in the landscape of Parkdale – the eateries, the local groceries that still mark the neighbourhood, and the newcomer and social services that have been available. One of my favourite Caribbean groceries, FullWorth, is still standing – and withstanding – near Queen and Lansdowne. I lived nearby and dropped in for groceries, but also furniture and even clothing. The fruit stands and flower shops on Queen West have been in the family businesses of immigrants for decades.

The neighbourhood also defined itself in its many happenings, and sometimes you just didn't know if something was going on until you fell upon it. And that's precisely what happened to me on that Masaryk-Cowan basketball court one day in 2007.

I had expected a quiet morning, actually. But when I walked in, I found the place teeming with Tibetan-Canadians. There were children running around, parents and elders speaking in the main-floor corridor and in the kitchen, light music playing on a stereo. I can still smell the coffee, tea, and refreshments being served to those who wanted it. Most of all, I remember the game taking place on that basketball court. Two teams with jerseys written with Tibetan script and colours, playing in full-court competition. The play wasn't exactly fluid, but that's beside the point.

The auditorium stage and the low rafters were packed with people looking on in curiosity and wonder. The refs, blowing their whistles and guiding the game, were hauling ass up and down the court, trying to keep up with the younger players. It was a scene, a real collision of community – a sight I can't forget to this day.

The Lungta Basketball Tournament, as the event was called, brings hundreds of Tibetan community members together – and has done so for years. Tibetans have been coming in waves to Toronto for decades. Many left China due to political tension, violence, and state oppression fuelled by the Tibetan region's desire for independence from China. From 1998 to 2008, according to a May 2008 story in the *Toronto Star*, about three thousand Tibetans moved to Toronto. Many of those arrivals call Little Tibet home. I wouldn't blame anyone for using that moniker, really: Parkdale is now home to the largest concentration of Tibetan newcomers in Canada.

This close-knit community sought the tournament as a safe space to come together again – when the pressures of daily life can drive people apart. After I worked out, I stuck around for hours that day, just taking it all in. I hadn't realized there were that many Tibetans in Parkdale. I saw how they'd found a way to engage with each other in a setting that one wouldn't imagine functioned as a binding agent. Basketball has become a connective tissue between generations of Tibetan-Canadians.

On that day, sports mattered.

• • •

Head into any gym – whether Masaryk-Cowan or the school court at Oakwood Collegiate, or the baseball diamonds at Leaside Park, the cricket pitches at Eglinton Flats – and you'll see it. Pick a place, any place, in the Greater Toronto Area that evokes memories: the time you played pickup basketball at the courts of Dufferin Grove Park, or that time you sat to watch kids, maybe even your own kids, play pickup hockey at Ted Reeve Community Arena. Think of each and every road run, either for charity or for your own health and well-being. The sights and sounds are unforgettable. The dribbles, the

Even if the ice has been removed for the summer, the rinks around the GTA are filled with, among other sports, ball hockey – including here, at South Fletchers Sports Complex in Brampton, ON. (Courtesy of Hockey 4 Humanity)

yelling and hollering, the ringing hollow of aluminum bats and hockey pucks; the smell of sunflower seeds and hockey sweat; the sheer joy on children's faces, the frustration of grown men wallowing in defeat; incredible dives for Frisbees and rugby touches.

At the best of times, sport – the act of organizing and playing with others – is the lifeblood of a place.

This city is the home of the Toronto Maple Leafs – not the century-old hockey team, but the baseball team that has been a tenant at Christie Pits Park for decades. Toronto has hosted numerous international sporting events – the Pan Am Games and its equivalent for para-athletes, numerous World Cups of hockey, and the World Baseball Classic, among others. The city has bid on two summer Olympics in the past and may do so again in the future.

These events or aspirations mark Toronto's sports identity on a macro level. But I'm more interested in the micro – the sports on the ground, the sports in people's hearts.

In this city, sport looks like the men, women, and children who live here, a place where disabled people can access facilities and women can connect in a place of no judgment and great care. Young Muslim girls in hijab and sneakers help their younger peers find basketball courts where they would be otherwise excluded or kept away.

Founded in 2017, the Hijabi Ballers project seeks to recognize and celebrate the athleticism of Muslim girls and women. They hold events and run programs in the city of Toronto. (Courtesy of Yasin Osman)

The places we see are a reflection of those who live here, and they encompass everything from the venues for the most popular games – basketball courts, hockey rinks, and baseball diamonds – to spaces for cool and niche sports and games – bocce courts, cricket wickets, roller derby rinks.

The city also strongly advocates for all to take part. The Toronto Accessible Sports Council consists of passionate volunteers who are directly involved in the adapted sports and recreation sector. TASC seeks to increase awareness and participation in sport and recreation within the city's disabled community. Their work resonates: they have helped many people find local accessible pools and advised on how to access them safely.

Sports have also brought the city to life in many ways. For me, the city's unique culture points to a healthy future – a place that is abundant in play can become the platform for teaching and leading others, and elevating the quality of life for all.

• • •

There's another side to this story. Sports matter because physical activity – moving, interacting with others – is an essential human function. To be physically active, but also to organize on a broad scale, means so much to our collective health and well-being.

Toronto ranks highly in terms of livability – it consistently makes the top ten of a list compiled by the Economist Intelligence Unit. Yet the city's livability is at risk because of escalating costs of living, fewer opportunities to purchase your first home, flattening real wages, precarious work, and the like. The barriers to sport are similarly stark.

We face not just a crisis of work and a crisis of living, but also a crisis of play. There's an interconnectedness here between sport and our daily lives that I want to explore.

These interconnected crises of livability disproportionately punish communities of colour and economically and socially marginalized people who come to Canada and Toronto looking to create a life that is satisfying for themselves, their loved ones, and their community.

The pandemic exposed and exacerbated the city's inequality. Communities of colour, low-wage workers, the elderly, and the disabled were more likely to contract COVID-19, to work on the front lines of health care and education, and to endure hardships, from anti-Asian discrimination to rent abuse by landlords. To rebuild equity, the city needs to consider how to deliver benefits to everyone, not just the well off.

In the context of these bigger battles, what lies ahead for Toronto's sports future?

We need to look at this question with fresh eyes. To build a thriving and inclusive sports culture, we need to learn from ourselves. During the pandemic, the loss of facilities and critical infrastructure, countless traditional and unconventional organized activities, forced us to realize what we had taken for granted before March 2020. I've seen a city desperately fight to keep the weekly soccer games alive, to make sure festival plans don't fall by the wayside. I saw folks pick up new activities and try to connect with others in a socially distant way.

I saw efforts by neighbourhoods and communities to change the way they think about streetscapes and the importance of parks. I saw how the fight to protect the vulnerable and marginalized has been so much more clear and present in Toronto – and beyond.

The pandemic also prompted a new way of thinking about open space, activity, sports, health, and what it means to be a citizen of a city. And so, I will look at the past and the present to help envision how our future should look. This is not just a basketball story. It is not just a hockey story. This is a story about the city, every city. But what do these challenges all tell me about Toronto? That people make a city, and the city's future is people-powered.

We're at a fork in the road. Is the future of our city – heck, practically any North American city – one in which only the people who pay can play, or is there a better path?

While the affluent and privileged have elite facilities and programming, communities convene and neighbourhoods continue to play. They get into the streets for hockey and basketball, whether it's illegal or not. Our culture is a product of our ideas, and if we want a sports culture that reflects Toronto's strongest aspirations – an accessible, diverse, multi-faceted place that truly looks like the Toronto we see in our dreams – then we will need to work at it.

Which means expanding definitions. 'When you talk about sports and community, it tends to get sucked into minor baseball, minor soccer, minor hockey, those kinds of leagues, swim clubs and that sort of thing,' Peter Donnelly, an expert on sports policy and politics at the University of Toronto's Faculty of Kinesiology and Physical Education, tells me. 'But if you think about that Bangladeshi community centre and what kind of things are happening there, then you really get into some interesting things – we found games being played in Toronto that I didn't know.' We need to create a livable, vibrant place that matches with the movements that we don't know about and yet plays a vital role in the civic growth of our city. And we must support communities in their search for space, belonging, and connection.

If we fail, we will need to reckon with the reality that Toronto's romantic ideals of inclusion, diversity, and multiculturalism are unfulfillable. And we will have to reconcile ourselves to the consequences of a sports culture divided among the haves and the have-nots.

We can't keep playing these games.

2

SAMI AND LOU

For Sami Hill, life on the basketball court is everything. Sami got her hands on a basketball early on. The Toronto native showed a gift for shooting at a young age, managing to stand out in a family stacked with athletes. Her dad, Samuel, played basketball for the University of Toronto Varsity Blues in the mid-1980s. Her brother, Alex, was a five-year player for those same Blues twenty years later and – at last check – is the program's all-time highest point scorer. Her younger sister, Kate, finished her college stint at La Salle University in Philadelphia. And her mom, Pamela, was a track star and former Canadian champion in triple jump. That's a lot of clout in a family that loves to play.

'Yeah, it was awesome to have all the people I played with growing up, and coaches and my family being able to be there and back in the gym, kind of where it all started. I guess I started getting serious about basketball in Grade 9 when I went to Eastern,' she says during a post–Pan Am Games training camp in Edmonton in 2019.

Objectively, Sami has shone brighter than them all. If basketball was her canvas, the ball was her brush, and she took full advantage of the opportunities to play. Sami joined her high school team at Eastern Commerce Collegiate Institute in 2008, with all the expectations in the world. She has gone on to play professionally in Germany and France and compete for Team Canada, in Olympic qualifiers and regional tournaments.

And these expectations are not heaped only on Sami. The school, located around the corner from a former 7-Eleven and steps from a subway station in Toronto's Danforth Village, has a reputation that extends across the city, the province, and the country. Eastern Commerce, 'E-Comm' to some, and officially the Eastern Saints, traces a basketball history and sporting tradition that dates as far back as World War I.

The school's athletic heyday began in 1974, when former vice-principal Lou Sialtsis made it his mission to bring high-performance basketball to a school of 1,300 kids. Eastern, extraordinarily, had only about a hundred boys attending by his account, and he wanted to provide extracurricular activities that appealed to them. Many came from farther reaches of the city and had been stuck in schools where students had few extracurricular options available. In those days, local kids had three high school choices – Eastern Commerce, Danforth Tech, and Riverdale Collegiate – and you only went to a collegiate if you planned to attend university (which was effectively academic streaming).

I first visited the school in 2015 as a freelance writer after years of reporting on high school athletics in the Greater Toronto Area. That experience was electrifying: as the fluorescent lights buzzed above in Eastern's gym, I watched the senior boys basketball team sprint end to end, employing an explosive mid- and long-range game. The ball didn't just swish, and the speed wasn't just blinding. The bleachers – these overhanging bleachers, which required spectators to walk up a couple flights of stairs, were packed with kids and teachers. The echoes were so loud they made it difficult to hear someone speaking in front of you. Those matches, at times, rivalled pro baseball games at the Rogers Centre or hockey at Maple Leaf Gardens and what was then called the Air Canada Centre. And they were the norm, as was the winning. E Comm won their first city title in 1976 and never looked back.

'Once we had a little bit of success, it snowballed,' Sialtsis tells me. I spoke with Lou years ago, for hours, about his time at Eastern, a place he left in 2002. He had so much to say, so many stories to share about the program.

With his baritone voice, calm demeanour, and strong positive aura, Lou is a brown-haired, bespectacled gentleman with a limitless passion for education and basketball. We spoke in 2015 for three hours, and Lou served up stories aplenty. He recalled, in crystal-clear detail, how the squad was one of the first Canadian high schools to really impress American competitors. In 1982, in New York City on an international trip, the team lost badly to Riverside Church, a New York–based amateur team that included eventual NBA players Chris Mullin, Mark Jackson, and Olden Polynice. But after that game, Eastern drew accolades for competing.

'When we lost that game, everyone came to us after and remarked on how well the team played; they were surprised by us,' recalls Sialtsis, who was on the sidelines that day.

He talked about the incredible alumni – like Simeon Mars, an exceptional high school player who came back to coach in the 1990s. In four seasons, Coach Mars won two provincial titles, compiled a 140–21 overall record, and had an undefeated season at 44–0 in the 1994–95 school year.

Players like Joe Alexander and Charles Rochelin had a meteoric rise in the eighties. David Joseph, the father of point guard Cory Joseph – himself a former Toronto Raptor – served as a long-time coach at Eastern. He eventually moved to Pickering, where he applied what he learned, developing basketball camps with local coaches that continue to this day. Cory and his brother Devoe won two Ontario Federation of Student Athletic Associations (OFSSA) championships with Pickering High School. David went on to be the head coach for the Mississauga Power of the National Basketball League of Canada and guided that squad to their first ever playoff appearance in the 2013–14 season.

At Eastern, the boys' and girls' basketball squads have collected more championships and medals than any other high school program in Ontario. The boys' and girls' teams have, combined, won ten OFSSA gold medals and five silvers since 1974. They have entered the tournament and competed for city championships in every year of its existence. (OFSSA holds annual provincial championships in numerous sports, including basketball. The association's membership, representing hundreds of schools and tens of thousands of students, is the largest of its kind in Canada and the second largest in North America, after California.) Eastern has pushed out a number of athletes who have gone on to achieve great things. Its most successful alumnus, Jamaal Magloire, played at Eastern and won two OFSSA gold medals before heading to the University of Kentucky, one of the undisputed heavyweights of the National Collegiate Athletic Association (NCAA) men's basketball. Magloire won a national championship there in 1998 and, to this day, remains the only Canadian to have won amateur championships in both Canada and the U.S.

In the NBA, Magloire was drafted in the top twenty by the Charlotte Hornets and went on to the all-star team in 2004. He's been an assistant coach with the Toronto Raptors for years now, sharing his offensive and defensive expertise with many of the team's power forwards and centres: Amir Johnson, Jonas Valančiūnas, and, recently, Pascal Siakam and Marc Gasol.

Until the mid-2000s, Eastern was primarily a hub for boys' basketball. Under the tutelage of Kareem Griffin and a group of coaches, the girls' program gained full-fledged support in 2005 from its administration to recruit broadly and grow. That focus paid off almost immediately as the Eastern Saints won their first provincial gold medal in girls' basketball at the OFSSA tournament in 2007.

Sami was part of that first wave of student athletes and won an OFSSA championship as a freshman in 2008. As older players graduated and moved on, she became the team's captain.

She took the captaincy to heart and, along with her teammates Bilie Grant and Vaneil Simpson, Eastern emerged as a triple threat. Speaking to the *Toronto Observer* in October 2011, she hedged on that description. The way Eastern was playing, she said, was a team effort.

'I don't think it's a Big Three,' Hill said. 'I think it's a Big Twelve or Thirteen, because we all have a significant role on the team and it's working out pretty well so far.'

Bilie Grant, Sami's power forward teammate, echoed that sentiment. 'There's no real selfishness on the team,' Grant told the *Observer*. 'There can be a different leading scorer every game and everyone's okay with it as long as we win, which is a really good team to be on.'

Their dominance in Toronto basketball circles was well documented. On November 1, 2011, Eastern showed substantial grit in a match against Oakwood Collegiate, the Barons.

The Eastern–Oakwood rivalry is and always will be a big draw. It dates back decades – fervent contests for both the boys' and girls' programs. Ask anyone with a long memory: that rivalry was unmatched anywhere in Ontario high school basketball.

A century-old school located on St. Clair West, in the Regal Heights neighbourhood, Oakwood sported its own basketball pedigree, with city-wide and provincial success that matched Eastern's. Each and every game, a regular season tilt after school, a regional playoff match, even city finals – they all had their share of fireworks. The games drew feverish crowds cheering on the players. The gameplay itself was rapid, with swift ball movement and physical rebounding. The games were played in gyms that, in some cases, had limited space. Eastern Commerce's court, for example, is famously small, with very little sideline room. Kids would fly around the court.

The games were well attended, the scores close. Picture yourself sitting in those wooden bleachers at Oakwood, listening to students howl for their squad, the reverberations of 'Defence, defence' coming in rapid succession. Parents, community members, and basketball nerds packed in to see these rivals go at it. And yes, many scouts came to see Sami ply her craft.

During that early November game, on Oakwood's home court, the team fielded some of their younger players. 'There wasn't really much to the scheme, we've played these guys twice already, and we know what they do – that made us successful the last game,' Coach Kareem Griffin says afterwards. The Saints wanted the full roster ready for OFSSA the next spring.

'Those girls, when it comes time for OFSSA, we're going to need them,' he adds. 'We had to incorporate them now to give them some minutes.'

The game had been close throughout. The Barons matched shot for shot, and had a 38–36 lead after three quarters. But Hill and company worked the court, played solid defence, and came out of it with a comfortable 56–40 win, with the Barons scoring very little in the last quarter.

'I think we just realized it was time to go, and if we wanted to win this game, we had to do everything we could in the last quarter because we let it be a close game the whole time,' Hill says.

The Big Three brought the goods over and over again: physical post play, tremendous range, a hunger and peskiness on defence. The Saints were equally respected and feared in basketball circles.

Sami appeared in the provincial championships every year they qualified. She had a tremendous high school and amateur career. Combined with a solid run at her North Toronto basketball club, where she won a U19 provincial championship – within the hotly competitive Ontario Basketball Association spring league, one of the most eye-popping amateur basketball leagues but composed of non-school-affiliated clubs – Sami was on her way, and her community was right there with her.

Since graduating from college, she's played in Germany and remains as motivated as ever to keep building on her pedigree. 'My career's been a testament to my hard work,' she tells me, after returning from the Pan Am Games in Lima, Peru. 'I was always seen as one of the better players on all the teams, but I don't think I was ever the best player – like in Ontario, in Canada – or the Player to Watch. I was never highly recruited out of school. I mean, I ended up getting to an amazing school and had a good career there. But I think I just kind of took this step-by-step pathway rather than being placed on the best team right away.

'There were small goals after small goals that I had to achieve to get here. So I think hard work has probably been my main thing and is the consistent thing going forward. That will help me continue to achieve my goals.'

When, in March 2013, she formally signed to play for Virginia Tech, in Blacksburg, Virginia, she knew she had to celebrate with the community that helped her get her chance to play pro. She went on to play all four years – and was a starter in her latter seasons with the Hokies.

And so, in an echoing gym during an early afternoon at the Eastern site, dozens of friends, students, family members, and coaches came together to hear where she would commit. I remember the day well because, to be completely honest, I was running late and they delayed the proceedings to make sure I got there in time. A little embarrassing, but they appreciated my role in spreading the word of her commitment.

Looking back at that day, Sami was ecstatic. 'Yeah, it was awesome to have all the people I played with growing up and coaches and my family being able to be there and back in the gym kind of where it all started.

'I started getting serious about basketball in Grade 9 when I went to Eastern,' she tells me. 'So it's pretty fun to be able to sign to Virginia Tech – where the future of my basketball would be – in the place where I kind of grew my game with all the people around me who helped me get to that point.'

As it happened, Sami didn't sign with Virginia Tech first. She committed to Yale University. 'I was caught up in the fact that going to Yale will be pretty awesome just because it's Yale,' she laughs. 'And about two weeks after I signed, I kept talking to my parents. They knew my basketball dream to be a professional beyond the Canadian national team and they asked me what school I thought would help me with my basketball goals. Would it be playing in the [Atlantic Coast Conference] at a big-time school, against the top basketball players in the country, or would it be going to Yale and having a great basketball career but being more focused on my studies?'

(The ACC is a collegiate athletic conference located in the eastern U.S., and operates with the NCAA. Its member universities represent a range of well-regarded private and public universities of different sizes, and many of those schools have become national champions in various sports – especially basketball. This conference features rival programs North Carolina, the collegiate home of Michael Jordan, and Duke University – that have a number of men's and women's basketball championships between them.)

'So I kind of took that all in and realized that I should be playing at Virginia Tech in the ACC if I wanted to take my basketball as far as I could possibly go,' Sami says.

She truly got a proper send-off. The ceremony included four other Eastern students who committed to various colleges and universities in the United States. There were speeches from teachers and Coach Kareem Griffin, and the players officially signed their commitment papers.

At the time, and you could even argue to this day, Eastern had placed more high school students in NCAA-affiliated schools than any other Canadian school, private or public.

It's impressive that a public school had the juice to do any of this, to get the attention of American institutions and signal that Canada could also ball while producing incredibly mature, grounded students who could excel in whatever field they chose.

It was a sight to behold. Too bad, because it was the last time a signing day ever happened.

3

THE END OF EASTERN

Two years after Sami's signing ceremony, Eastern Commerce closed. The Toronto District School Board shuttered the International Baccalaureate stream there. And the basketball program, an international powerhouse and an example followed by high schools across Canada, ceased to exist. Full closure had long been rumoured – a concern shared by students and staff for years. In its last days, the school was a study in contrasts. The building in those final weeks was largely quiet and empty. Many corridors were literally closed off because they weren't occupied by students or staff. The class sizes were in the single digits, and there wasn't much of a school culture outside that gym. But once you entered the upper-floor atrium overlooking the court, the poetry of basketball was on display.

Ultimately, the school closed due to budget issues – too few resources for a technical school and not enough students to justify the funding. Eastern had sixty-two kids enrolled during that final year. Without a Grade 9 class for two years, and with enrollment numbers dwindling, the school board had no choice.

'There hasn't been a Grade 9 program, or even a Grade 10 program, at the school,' says Nigel Tan, who, at the time, headed Eastern's phys. ed department.

Much of the funding available to the school was still devoted to running a basketball program and helping its remaining students get to post-secondary school. Competitively, they wanted to play with Canadian and American collegiate basketball programs.

Tan, who served as the senior team's assistant basketball coach, understood that the writing was on the wall. '[The players] knew they were going to have to finish their four, five years as part of the program, and the guys who came in later, in Grade 10 and 11, those were pieces that were added on later so they weren't considered to be somebody we would be staying open for.'

Looking back, Eastern made quite the mark. But it was the educators' work off the court that really defined the spirit of the school. Starting a boys' basketball program back in the 1970s had not just been a ploy to keep kids busy and occupied. Basketball was the school's educational identity, and core to the plan.

The program itself was an education, not just an extracurricular activity. Sialtsis, and the many coaches over the years, made it their mission to whip players into shape academically. With the help of teachers and support staff, he instituted a study hall before practice and set strict standards for grades and play, a system that continued until its end and is practised at other schools to this day.

'When I mean identity, it's the kind of palette of opportunities that the students would create in school [which was] further enhanced by having this program,' he tells me. Many of the players leveraged their own skills and intelligences and carried that forward in the team and elsewhere. 'That's one big thing I feel needs to be said: this is not a school that should be defined by it, but it might become defined by the basketball, whether it's for good or bad.'

The Eastern model for education saw many kids graduate with honours and go on to post-secondary degrees from major Canadian and American schools. They now work in a variety of fields and give back to the community through basketball. Many of these kids, young boys of colour, were perceived to be 'difficult' or 'challenging' to teach. Those stereotypes, however, don't align with the stories of the hundreds of alumni who graduated and moved on to do great things. Some of those kids came from neighbourhoods with reputations unfairly tethered to crime and danger – places like Regent Park, Malvern, Jane and Finch.

Lou Sialtsis's memories of basketball at Eastern have not gone away and they never will.

'Those of us who are a part of this, or appreciate it, we celebrate the successes we have,' he says. Lou left the school in the early 2000s and retired for good in 2004. 'They ask me how I felt, and I say I've been away from Eastern, I was transferred to Birchmount Park Collegiate. But I never left Eastern. My heart is still there.'

• • •

Dwayne Sybliss's heart is still at Eastern, too. He was a student and then became a coach for a number of years. For Dwyane, thoughtful, tall in stature, with kind eyes, Eastern was such an important beacon for basketball.

'Eastern was really interesting because [it was] different than any other school that I can really remember,' Dwayne says to me. 'They really had a plan – I want to say 'plan,' but it's not a plan. They had a strategy that was in place.'

Dwayne remembers how, when he was younger, Eastern would host elementary schools from around the GTA and allow them to watch the senior boys' team – a collection of Grade 10, 11, and 12 kids – during practice.

'You see the senior guy – you're seeing Jamaal [Magloire], you're seeing Colin [Charles], you're seeing all these guys and they're decked out in Champion gear and shoes, and everything is coordinated. And you're like, wow, "I want to be a part of this – they're guys in the NBA, right?"'

Now a filmmaker, coach, and entrepreneur, Dwayne is doing some serious scene-setting when we speak. He says it could be difficult to describe the Eastern experience to incoming students. Some felt it was humbling; Dwayne did. 'You might have been the best player on your local elementary school team scoring thirty, forty points a game, but now you're buying into a culture – you're buying into what it means to be a team.

'A lot of us didn't understand that we wanted to be a part of it,' Dwayne adds. Eastern was a landing place for elite basketball kids from across the city – places like Lawrence Heights, Jane and

Finch, Malvern, and Regent Park. Kids from far-flung communities, with varying ideas about themselves and others, were introduced to one another in Eastern's corridors and on its basketball court. 'The one thing Eastern did for me, and a lot of my other friends, it was able to break down those walls,' he says.

There were no neighbourhood beefs there. The international language, in that gym and that classroom, was ball. 'It was kind of like ... you might have hated a dude from Flemo,' says Dwayne, referring to Flemingdon Park, a multicultural, multilingual neighbourhood located in the Don Mills and Eglinton area. 'But if he gave you a nice pass, and you finished that layup, you had to give him respect – or that nod or that high five – to let him know, like, "Yo, that was a good pass."'

All of this bonding, this connection-building, was organic. 'And the one thing they'd stress – and I think most schools do it now – is how academics are so in line with your current athletic ability, and always wanting to need to kind of get better at wanting to grow on and off the court,' says Dwayne.

'Can you operate within the system? Can you function in the classroom? Can you be a good person when you're not in school? Quickly, you begin to see guys start to drop off. And then, you know, you work with the guys who you've been there with for four years.'

Eastern proved to be a great experience for Dwayne. It taught him a lot about how basketball skills – even the ones on the court – could transfer to real life. '[It was] a culture that would always whisper in our ears, like, you know, "the tougher the battle, the sweeter the victory,"' he says. 'They would always say, "You know, fatigue makes cowards of us all." They would always whisper this.'

With that knowledge, Eastern killed the competition. For decades. But never again.

• • •

While the school may be shuttered for good, Eastern's essence, its teachings, haven't vanished. The building now houses the school board's archives as well as the Kapapamahchakwew – Wandering Spirit School, devoted to Indigenous children.

The people who made Eastern what it was went on to apply that knowledge elsewhere – with great results. For example, I'll begin with one person, a man I respect dearly. In basketball circles, they call him Mac. During my reporting, I just called him Coach.

Kevin Jeffers, a man with a quick wit and a small, silver crucifix around his neck, grew up in Regent Park, a short distance from Eastern. When he joined the Eastern program as an assistant in the early 2000s, he learned a great deal from his boss – then head coach Roy Rana. (Roy has gone on to do great things since leaving Eastern in the late 2000s, including head coaching duties at Ryerson University, helping Canada Basketball win international gold, and ongoing work in the NBA.)

What Mac saw in that Eastern program was crystal clear: support, discipline, energy. It was about basketball as a vehicle for something more.

'Basketball's a tool to reach these guys, but if it's the only tool and that's the only drive, then you understand right away that these guys are not going to make it,' says Mac, who coached the boys in 2015. 'We try to instill good character and hold them accountable through all that stuff that other programs may overlook.'

It was Eastern's character-building, educationally intense regimen that moved Jeffers to his next major job: head coaching a prep school program at Central Tech, one of the city's oldest high schools.

For decades, the neighbourhood around Central Tech, a century-plus-old castle of a school near Bathurst and Bloor, has been a hub for Black Canadians who not only live close by but also have built successful businesses and professional community there. Many children from those families attend Central Tech.

Contrast, a Black-owned and -run newspaper founded by Denham Jolly, a prolific and highly respected Jamaican-Canadian businessman, was based in the area, as was Lloyd's Barber Shop, where my dad and I would get haircuts. I used to buy doubles – small, exceptionally delicious Trinidadian snacks made of fried dough, chickpea, and curry – at the Caribbean Roti Palace, a stone's throw from the famous Honest Ed's discount department store. Growing up downtown, I visited the area frequently for appointments with our family doctor or to help my mom look for bargains at Honest Ed's. For a time, I worked in the neighbourhood as a community news reporter.

Central Tech has its own rich sports history, too. Going back decades, young athletes from Tech have been a part of local and Canadian history. Writing in the *Annex Gleaner*, Justin Viviera told the story of Samuel 'Sam' Richardson, a sprinter who ran alongside the famed American sprinter Jesse Owens at the 1936 Olympic Games in Berlin, Germany. Richardson, who before Central Tech attended school at King Edward Public School and Lord Lansdowne Public School, finished fifth with the Canadian men's 4×100-metre relay team and finished fourteenth and twentieth in the long and triple long jumps.

'I'll always remember his grace and the feeling of pride once I found out who he was and what he accomplished,' his son, Stacey Richardson, told the *Gleaner* in 2017. 'When I think about him, I'm always revisited by the gratification I grew up with from my father and his accolades.'

Richardson also won the gold medal in long jump in London at the 1934 British Empire Games (now known as the Commonwealth Games). At that time, he was the youngest competitor to ever win a gold medal in track.

Richardson later set a Canadian record of twenty-five feet in the long jump at the Canadian Track and Field Championships in Winnipeg in 1935 – a record that wouldn't be broken for twenty-five years. After his athletic career ended, Richardson joined the CBC in 1955, working as a stagehand for *The Wayne and Shuster Show* and *Mr. Dressup*, the children's television show.

• • •

It was the school's rich history that drew Coach Jeffers when he signed on as coach in 2017. He had been approached by a number of public and private institutions, all looking for someone to turn their programs into powerhouses. After Eastern closed, he seriously considered walking away from coaching altogether – he tells me he had accomplished just about everything he wanted at Eastern. But he was drawn back to the game because Central Tech offered a challenge he couldn't refuse.

'It's breaking down the school's stigma,' he says. 'You hear about Central Tech, you google it, the first thing you're gonna see is lockdowns, shootings, and violence. It's their parents trusting in the decision they're making that "You know what, we're going to make this program amazing."'

The stigma goes back decades, and I'd seen it for myself as a reporter with the *Annex Gleaner*. Central had been the focus of a few incidents, although not all of them were directly linked to the school. At that time, in late September and early October 2010, there had been four shootings in close succession, each leading to lockdowns. Parents and the community worried about safety and the students' well-being.

A lot of those concerns were aired during an October 2010 public meeting at the Bickford Centre, a nearby educational facility. Toronto police inspector David Vickers and Detective Sergeant Brian Kelly said that investigations were progressing, but the police still need help gathering information.

'It's important for you to know that the victims of the gun violence, almost 100 per cent of them, are people who live lifestyles that are consistent with violence. I'm talking drug dealing, gang violence, putting themselves in positions, relationships, and conflicts that cause these types of gun violence incidents to occur,' said Vickers. 'I'm happy to say that citizens are not being gunned down on the street.'

Happy to know, but those incidents reinforced the stigma that had given Central Tech the wrong label for years. The truth is that crime doesn't define Tech; the people do.

In 2013, for example, the death of Tyson Bailey, a Central Tech Blues football player, sent waves of sadness through the community. The media reports barely covered anything besides the crime and the pain.

Bailey, who became the starting running back as a Grade 10 student for Central Tech, and also played football for the Metro Toronto Wildcats, was poised to compete in the Ontario Varsity Football League that season. The OVFL is the province's largest youth amateur football league, and many of its kids go on to play collegiate-level football throughout Canada – and, if they're lucky, the U.S.

But Tyson didn't have a chance to do that. He was killed in his Regent Park apartment building on January 18, 2013 – shot several times while visiting a friend. The case is open, and the police have never arrested or charged a suspect.

The community – including Central Tech – refused to be defined by such violence. When Tyson's life was celebrated shortly after, the community – his Central Tech community, the local youth football community, and his loving friends and family – sought to celebrate and uplift one another. They also began to build Tyson's legacy: his youth football club, the Metro Toronto Wildcats, renamed its player assistance fund in his memory.

'When you really get slapped in the face with this, when it's a kid that you know and been talking to who was so excited to be part of what you been working on for fifteen years, this type of thing really hits home,' Wildcats president Chuck Richardson tells me.

The fund in Tyson's name supplements expenses for kids who can't afford to play football. Started in 2012 by junior varsity coach Ed Babin and his wife, Cathy Rober, who gave $10,000, the fund has attracted matching donations and other contributions ever since. Dozens of young football players in the GTA have received funding in its run.

When Richardson and the Wildcats renamed the scholarship program in Tyson's honour, I cried. I didn't know Tyson or his family, but seeing that kind of support where Tyson was at his happiest made me shed tears of joy. I see myself in kids like Tyson, and I look up to non-profits like the Wildcats, whose members take care of each other.

When Coach Jeffers saw he had a chance to make a different impact on students at Central Tech, on the very kids he would see in his own community, it was a no-brainer. And his efforts, to this day, have been resounding.

Many kids from neighbourhoods like Regent Park and Malvern have gone on to attend major basketball programs in Canada and the U.S. For example, Jamal Fuller, nicknamed 'Lay Lay' by Coach Jeffers and the community, committed to Hill College in Hillsboro, Texas. Eugene Kanku, a guard who was also part of Coach Jeffers's first wave of athletes, joined Cape Breton University in 2018 and transferred to Brock University in 2021.

Some, like Evan Shadkami, decided to stay and compete in Toronto. A six-foot-one guard, Evan was part of the first wave of kids in Coach Jeffers's program. Far more than just a room set up in a gym, Central Tech Blues XXXI is a prep program established by the school and sponsored by Jordan-brand apparel. The program's main facility was one of a few gyms in Central Tech, and had been refurbished with slogans painted on the walls. The place is a shiny gem, if you ever have a chance to check it out.

The players, including Evan, had known Coach Jeffers through their involvement in the Ontario Basketball Association, an amateur organization that fields some of the most competitive play in the province. The OBA's membership consists of private basketball clubs and is arranged by age groups. Evan played with Mac's club, called Peoples Basketball, which functioned like a charity that teaches life skills to young men. Before closing in 2020, Peoples gave plenty of young players incredible exposure to elite-basketball training.

Evan, a crafty guard with incredible shooting ability, was so open-minded when he arrived at the program, he knew what to expect. By reputation, Mac brings tough love and plenty of volume to his practices. The noise of the dribbling basketballs and squeaking shoes are matched only by Mac's raised voice.

Walking among the scrimmaging players, Mac alternates between encouragement ('Yes, that's what I'm looking for!') and criticism ('Why? Why did you make that pass?').

He was 'breaking them down and building them up,' Mac explains to me just prior to their inaugural season. 'It's nowhere where we want to be, but November's early.'

Evan got it. 'On the court, he's holding you accountable; if you do something wrong, he'll tell you about it. If you do it right, he'll tell you about it,' he tells me. 'He is always motivating you and he makes you really disciplined. When he yells at you, you can tell it's for your own good. He wants you to get better.' Evan shone during his senior year. His squad competed in the OBSA, where they reached the final. Evan himself was eventually named a CityTV Player of the Week, and his performance landed him a spot with the Varsity Blues, with the University of Toronto – just down the street from his high school alma mater. There, he was named to the All-Rookie Team for the Blues' conference, Ontario University Athletics.

The prep program at Central Tech is now an unstoppable force, making its own change at the school and in the lives of these young boys and girls.

Unfortunately, not every kid gets to run with a major school team. Or a club team. Or any team, for that matter.

In fact, it is harder than ever to play anywhere. Many families can't afford sports. Semi-professional athletes and leagues are scooping access to playing facilities. Along with their other difficulties, communities of colour can't find spaces to play. And while progress has been made, women and girls are not being brought into organized sports, and the disabled have few to no options to get active.

And we're not doing enough to push back against it.

4

NINE MEN IN A PARKING LOT

Kensington Market is one of my favourite Toronto neighbourhoods. I hold it in high regard for several reasons. For generations, Kensington has been a microcosm of the range of people who live in Toronto: merchants from Latin American groceries to a Filipino community centre and independent bike shops; residents ranging from artists and musicians to academics; and the landmarks, from Bellevue Square Park, one of my favourite hangouts, to Graffiti Alley, which is a joy to the eyes. Tom's Place has made many formal and semi-formal suits for friends of mine. Blue Banana Market is a great place to get someone a small token of appreciation. Veggie D'Light is one of my favourite vegan restaurants in Toronto (and I say this as a non-vegan – their food is supremely delicious).

In the early 2000s, the 'hood began closing its streets to cars on weekends as a way to animate the market area. Pedestrian Sundays has turned into a festival version of itself that even went on full display during the 2020 wave of the coronavirus, getting folks into the streets to support businesses trying to survive capacity restrictions.

But this place, like many neighbourhoods in the city, is dealing with constant growing pains: the gentrification of its buildings, businesses, and public spaces has created polarizing debates over how the neighbourhood should look, what businesses can operate in the market, and what kind of property development should take place here. The city is trying to figure out how to use heritage policies to protect Kensington from being washed away by development pressures.

One of the things I hope their work preserves is a feature of the neighbourhood that isn't bounded by four walls and a ceiling: it is the curious subculture of nine-man volleyball, a game that is a marvel for the eyes and ears, and one that regularly transforms Kensington's open spaces – mostly schoolyards like Lord Lansdowne public school, but there are stories of games shutting down streets in the neighbourhood – into places of culture, energy, and competition. I remember catching old footage of matches on YouTube – it's an incredible sensory experience. There are feverish crowds that pack courtside to watch. The players – laden in colourful ensembles and varying skills and backgrounds – are so competitive, not a single one likes to lose. The leaping ability of the players is jaw-dropping. Every spike is hit with authority, like the ball did something to them.

Fielding nine players per team, this sport can be played indoors or outdoors, on courts that are longer and wider than conventional volleyball. The game is fluid and quite chaotic, too, with three lines of players diving and sliding to defend their zones and manoeuvring to spike volleyballs with intent and killer instinct. The rules aren't anything I've ever seen, either. Unlike conventional volleyball, there are only three designated servers per match. Some players have special defensive or offensive roles and don't serve at all. You can't even jump on a serve!

But nine-man volleyball isn't just a game. This sport is intimately tied to Chinese diasporic history in ways that intrigue me but also may raise an eyebrow.

The sport arrived in North America with Chinese-American immigrants during the Depression, as workers used it to connect to fellow newcomers. The first intercity games were held in 1935 between squads from Boston and Providence, Rhode Island.

Ursula Liang, a journalist and filmmaker, has written extensively about the game. 'When the community was a Bachelor Society (men outnumbered women four-to-one) at a time when anti-Chinese sentiment and laws like the Chinese Exclusion Act forced Chinese restaurant workers and laundrymen to socialize exclusively amongst themselves, nine-man offered both escape and fraternity for men who were separated from their families in China and facing extreme discrimination and distrust,' says Liang, on her film's Kickstarter campaign.

That 1938 exhibition has, over decades, turned into the North American Chinese Invitational Volleyball Tournament (NACIVT), with teams coming from across the diaspora. Every Labour Day weekend, the nine-man world converges in one bustling event. The last NACIVT before the coronavirus pandemic, the seventy-fifth annual tournament, took place in Toronto at the Metro Toronto Convention Centre. Hundreds of players (159 teams!) attended, including a number of Canadian squads from Toronto and Vancouver.

Liang's documentary film *9-Man* shows how a powerful human force has moved within Chinatowns across the continent. 'I discovered nine-man in the late 1990s when my brother started playing,' she says. 'It was this amazing community where guys had confidence, swagger, height, and muscles – all things that defied stereotypes of Asians. This, of course, was way before [NBA stars] Jeremy Lin and Yao Ming. We had been raised in the suburbs and this connection to Chinatown and its own warrior-sport gave us something to be especially proud of as Chinese-Americans.'

Liang's passion for the game runs deep. 'As I moved on to a career as a sports journalist, I held especially tight to this spirited image of Asian men,' she added, on her Kickstarter. 'To put it bluntly, mainstream sports coverage is not friendly to the APA [Asian Pacific American] community – it's full of long-held ideas that reinforce the notion that Asian athletes are inherently inferior.'

Her film shows how nine-man is streetball – a gruelling sport played not just in parking lots but also on basketball courts, in industrial parks and schoolyards. Or, as Liang says in the film, 'on top of asphalt and broken glass.' The game connects generations of people, and the film does incredible justice to these men – showing the moments of camaraderie, the brutal scrapes, the ecstatic yells. Losing players never hide their disgust at being defeated. Shoulders are massaged, high-fives exchanged.

For the documentary, Liang spoke to a ninety-one-year-old man who had had three strokes but still had the strength to tell his story. Work, he said, was 'a long grind, six days a week.' 'Can you blame us for playing like crazy when we had a chance?' he asks. 'That took all the stress away, the loneliness.'

Canadians are not excluded from her story, which features Toronto Connex, one of the best nine-man squads in recent decades. They weren't the first local squad to win the NACIVT – Toronto Flying Tigers did that during the thirty-seventh edition, in 1981. That team's pure intensity has been present in Toronto nine-man circles for years.

It certainly affected Jeff Chung. He is one of the most successful Toronto volleyballers to ever grace a court. Before he became the Connex coach, he made a large impact as a player, first as a member of the University of Toronto Varsity Blues, and later on a provincial all-star squad, and finally the Canadian men's team. He's been provincial championship MVP three times, in 1996, 1997, and 1998, and won four Ontario gold medals in the nineties. Chung currently teaches and coaches within the Toronto District School Board. But his path to volleyball success came via nine-man. He was introduced to volleyball at a young age by a father who was trying to break down stereotypes.

'He actually encouraged sport at a very young age,' Chung says. 'He was very athletic himself. Long story short, he actually wanted me to be a basketball player, but somehow I fell in love with volleyball.'

His taste for nine-man grew from watching his dad play in Chinatown. 'When he stopped playing,' Chung recalls, 'he brought me to watch my eldest cousin on my mother's side – who was a Flying Tiger back then. The Flying Tigers were one of the top clubs and also one of the older clubs in Toronto.'

The Flying Tigers, Connex, and a third squad, Ngun Lam, have dominated North American nine-man in recent years. Since the

Tigers' first championship in 1981, these three clubs have won twenty-five NACIVTs. Connex, with Chung at the helm, has triumphed in five NACIVTs since 2008. Many of the tournament finals, in fact, have featured all-Canadian matchups. Connex actually won the 2019 NACIVT at the Metro Toronto Convention Centre. They outlasted 158 other teams – a massive win.

Chung really bought into volleyball after seeing his cousin Mike play for the Tigers. As a kid growing up in Chinatown near College and Spadina, he had a hearty introduction to nine-man. He played in Chinatown parking lots and at some of the local schools: Ogden Junior Public School and Lord Lansdowne Junior and Senior Public School, both nearby.

'Our connection to everyone was just in that neighbourhood, that whole pocket,' says Chung, who went on to play volleyball for Harbord Collegiate. 'I just pursued the sport accidentally, but it took me to the next level. At the same time, I would continue with nine-man in the summer. So as I grew on the sort of "normal side" of volleyball, nine-man was always there every summer for me.'

Volleyball and nine-man take up so much space in Jeff's heart. But there's an issue I want to address – and if we're to understand what inclusivity (and creating space) means in the Toronto context, addressing it and understanding it are essential to how we learn about the cultural dynamics of many local communities.

When you look at films or photos of nine-man, there are no non-Asian players. Women don't take up much space here, either. 'We used to call the other volleyball "sissyball,"' one player says in Liang's documentary. 'This was something that was uniquely ours. It was a game that was played by Chinese men.'

NACIVT rules dictate that, at any given time, each team must have at least six players on the court who are of Chinese descent. The remaining three players must be Asian. That was the rule. That is still the rule.

Is this a problem at all – an apparent 'exclusivity' issue? Some may say that excluding other ethnic groups is problematic.

Imagine if the rule meant only white players can play, for example. Others may argue that these leagues stunt the growth of high-performance players.

I had to sort out my feelings about nine-man's rules, so I spoke to Yuka Nakamura, a professor from York University's School of Kinesiology and Health Science. Nakamura is an authority on the nine-man subculture and has written about it in her book *Playing Out of Bounds: 'Belonging' and the North American Chinese Invitational Volleyball Tournament*.

For Nakamura, there are a lot of concerns: whether the rule is divisive, if the tournament is a safe space, and even whether the rule creates a space that favours better players over others – assuming one can move into mainstream sport once they have the skills or develop the courage to step out of their own community. 'I'm very uncomfortable with that assumption,' she tells me.

'Many of these organizations that run sport along ethnic lines or religious lines, people have a foot in both – they're participating in rec league, they're participating in Toronto sport and social clubs, but they're also playing with their mosque.'

Nakamura has long studied how sport is organized around ethnic or religious lines. What she has observed in nine-man reminds her of what she sees in some other sports. With volleyball, she noticed some really high-calibre athletes 'playing varsity or national teams or the Olympics, but also playing in nine-man.'

And then she says something that makes me reflect more closely about such sports. 'What was so important about these spaces is that [they welcomed] those individuals who couldn't access sport through the mainstream sport system – it could have been because of discrimination, because of limited opportunities, or it simply could be because they just didn't understand the sports system.'

While the worlds of ball hockey and basketball have lots of flexibility and a range of player skill and talent, spaces like hockey don't allow for the openness, in my opinion – even though those sports attract many casual participants.

'A lot of people don't understand the sport system in Canada and the relationship between clubs and rep leagues – and provincial and national sports organizations,' says Nakamura. 'These ethnic leagues and teams become really important spaces, not just for community building, but for skill development in sport as well.'

This is nothing new. If Caribbean immigrants are coming to bowl on a cricket pitch or put together youth basketball clubs for hundreds of kids, that kind of activity is as much of a tradition as marking a religious holiday. Sports are so important in these communities (with a long history), and its practice is nothing new to them. 'It just hasn't really been talked about and it's only now starting to be uncovered in a more focused way,' Nakamura says.

Talking more openly about how communities organize and prioritize their lives within our urban world can really improve how Torontonians engage in sports in this city. Believe me: the matter of whether traditions, customs, and conventions will suffer or disappear, or yield to some compromise, is an important question to consider.

For example, for a period, bocce – a lawn bowling-esque game perfected by Italians – was very well accommodated by local parks and rec agencies here post–World War II, littering much of the city with the ninety-one-by-thirteen-foot courts. Its massive presence in Toronto is a reflection of high levels of immigration from Italy and elsewhere. But now many of those courts aren't used because the old-timers have died or moved away.

In a course Professor Nakamura instructs, one about integration and culture, her students go into communities, including bocce circles, to interview people about their activities and the links to culture and identity – whether it's a league organized by a religious institution, competitive ones built up by elders in an apartment block or city block, or programmatic ones like in martial arts or soccer.

'One group that went and interviewed participants at a bocce club talked to them about the change in the participants and how they know that the next generation of players is not going to be their children or grandchildren,' she says, citing the Italian-created game.

The conversations always went to how groups were going to protect or ensure that bocce, or whatever other sport practice, continued, Nakamura explains. A lot of the answers to that question lay around 'bringing in new people and introducing it to people who are not of Italian background,' she says. 'Questions around tradition, authenticity, and purity might come into that but also the celebration of inclusion and the intercultural interaction comes in there, too.'

The nine-man heritage rule, which dates back only to the 1990s, exists within a larger debate. There are invariably going to be tensions about who belongs in a community, says Nakamura. Those stress lines even trace through Chinese communities. 'I devote a section [in *Playing Out of Bounds*] where I talk about mixed-race athletes. Players where one parent is Chinese but the other isn't are not considered Chinese within the tournament.'

Still, the rule is tricky because it's an exercise in balancing the celebration of sport as something that brings people together while also maintaining boundaries around cultural preservation. 'I wanted to explain why people would play in this tournament, despite the fact that there are very harsh physical conditions in some cases, and also because it can be really exclusionary,' says Nakamura. 'The exclusion is almost so much more heartbreaking because players feel such a tremendous sense of belonging at the same time,' she adds.

'So it's even more hurtful because you're welcomed on one hand and [you're] then being pushed away.'

5

WHY DO THE COURTS SUCK IN A CITY IN LOVE WITH BASKETBALL?

The Raptors championship parade in June 2019 was a magical moment for Toronto – the end result of what it meant to unite behind a worthy cause. A lot has been written and said about the team's impact beyond the sport itself. The Raptors' success gave the Canadian economy some bounce, grew participation rates in sports, and inspired more kids to aim to play at a high level.

As Gamal Abdel-Shehid, an associate professor at York University's School of Kinesiology and Health Science, notes, the team 'cemented themselves into the fabric and psyche of the city.' In a column in *The Conversation*, he observed that 'the Raptors have also succeeded in telling their story from the point of view of individuality and hard work. Many of the team's icons have embodied hard work and beating the odds, but also a dedication to greater causes than basketball. As much as the on-court success, it's translated into a groundswell of civic pride previously unseen. It is a marvel to watch.' From Masai Ujiri, the president of the team, to its roster during that unforgettable year, the team reflected a lot of what Toronto is: a convergence of ideas and people from all over the globe that thrived when they worked together.

With that awareness, basketball in Greater Toronto took on a different meaning. And it wasn't just about professional sports. But soon after the parade and the cheering ended, that sense of awakening was overtaken by something far less attractive yet galvanizing.

•   •   •

Luke Galati, a young Toronto filmmaker, is proud to call South Riverdale his home. 'I grew up on a street south of Pape and Danforth. I'm really grateful that I've been able to live in this neighbourhood. I feel like it has like a little of everything – you know, there's parks all around me, nice restaurants on the Danforth, the local grocery stores that I go to.' Within this urban home base, near Earl Grey Senior Public School, is a basketball court – a space that may as well have Galati's name on it. 'I went there basically every day – every evening, every weekend, I'd be out there,' he recalls. To my eye, Luke's devotion to that hardtop cathedral was like daily mass. He met his best friends there, he played with total strangers and neighbours down the street. 'It is really just an amazing place where everyone would just come after school or in the evenings.' Sacred ground.

One day soon after that Raptors championship parade in 2019, he was shocked to see that the city had taken down the basketball nets, despite the groundswell of interest in the sport from kids and adults alike. He knew the nets at many other courts nearby had also been taken down over the years. 'It always kind of rubbed me the wrong way,' he says.

The ironies pile up. During the Raptors championship parade, he was walking by the court and saw a family and some kids hanging out. 'They were literally shooting on a backboard that had no rim,' Galati says. 'I just thought that was so wrong.'

Galati's love of basketball beats as strongly as his love for his 'hood. He played competitively for years: Ontario Basketball Association hoops with East York, high school ball at Riverdale Collegiate, summer camps galore, and Amateur Athletic Union (AAU) ball with the Northern Kings, which fields kids who live in that part of the city. Luke got onto the Kings' squad out of sheer chance, he says.

It goes without saying that the game has given him so much. 'Growing up, going to my local courts playing basketball was like the best way to get to know my neighbours,' he recalls. 'And it was an amazing way to get to know people who are from my street but also who are down the street, the people who maybe have more money than me, people who have less money than me – it's kind of like the great equalizer.'

His love of the sport even drove him into sports journalism, which eventually led him to make a documentary about the legendary Eastern Commerce program. His forty-minute film, *Eastern*, was filmed over a year, just before the school retired the program. Galati describes the film, which won a 2016 award for best short documentary at the Toronto Short Film Festival, as 'the little engine that could.' It was eventually screened at the Toronto International Film Festival Lightbox. He's proud of how *Eastern* resonated. But it was Luke's next endeavour that really got the city's attention.

• • •

There are hundreds of basketball courts in the city. After Galati made some inquiries with the Toronto District School Board, he learned that the nets – like most outdoor nets in summer hours – come down after a certain time of the day. In the case of his local court, the two nets came down like clockwork at 3:00 p.m. But in some cases, including the courts at Earl Grey, the board took down the rims in response to noise complaints from local residents. In light of the Raptors' victory and the years he'd spent making connections to the community on those surfaces, Galati decided to do something: 'I'm like, "Enough is enough." I have to actually act on this, and I have to do something to change it.'

Toronto's neighbourhoods have all sorts of basketball courts with crumbling curbs, sunken asphalt, or sewer grates at centre court. You don't see that kind of neglect on baseball diamonds or in hockey arenas. Nor do any basketball courts have adjacent tuck shops or change rooms or washrooms.

I wonder: how is it that funding and programming for hockey in richer neighbourhoods is prioritizeed over funding for new courts and community programming in lower-income neighbourhoods with more newcomers and racialized residents? This is classic white supremacy – not the blatant, white-hood-wearing white supremacy of the Ku Klux Klan, but rather a system that collectively enables white people to maintain power over people of other races. Those systems are social, political, and economic. In the political thinking behind the organization of sports in Toronto, the planning certainly centres whiteness and economic power.

While none of this is news to Galati, he decided to focus his energy on rims. Using his filmmaking skills, he shot a video of board crews taking down the nets and then started a petition to lobby the city to change the policy. The petition – which is still online – painted a pretty stark picture of the circumstances:

> Currently at Earl Grey Sr. Public School, they have two basketball backboards on the TDSB Property. There's one big problem with the status quo though. The rims (the actual hoops) are removed once school ends at 3 p.m. The net that was a constant up & broke down after years was never fixed, leaving no where to play basketball outside for the community. This means that after school hours, in the evenings & weekends – kids in the neighbourhood can't play here. I want to change this & help provide the next generation & anyone from the neighbourhood the same constructive outlet that made a huge difference in my life. I know the difference that basketball & something as simple as a basketball net to play at can have on a young person's life.

The petition attracted several thousand signatures, plus a massive amount of media attention. Many in the city's sports communities amplified Galati's campaign.

The City of Toronto reacted swiftly with a statement:

Over the years, the City has attempted to balance the rights of everyone to enjoy Toronto's parks – and play basketball – with the rights of residents adjacent to those parks when it comes to noise.

The removal of basketball hoops in some parks, however, has created an imbalance. Not all basketball courts in parks have their hoops removed in the evening, just those in close proximity to homes. But removing basketball hoops at 6 p.m., as we saw in the video posted last night, is not reasonable. The City fully acknowledges this.

Effective immediately, therefore, the City – in consultation with Mayor Tory's office – has suspended the removal of basketball hoops from its parks so residents can continue to enjoy a game of basketball into the evening. The City encourages the use of its parks and being active, for young and old alike.

Staff will monitor noise complaints the City may receive on a case by case basis in an attempt to ensure everyone is free to enjoy both their parks and their backyards.

The petition worked. Luke used his platform to shine a light on something small that could, nonetheless, have a tremendous impact on communities around the city. He says that the issue resonated with many people in many neighbourhoods. But the public reaction – as well as similar stories that surfaced on social media from many other parts of the GTA – provided an eye-opening moment, and inspiration for his next projects. 'Sometimes, like when a whole group of people feels marginalized or feels like no one's listening to them,' he says, 'sometimes we just need one little spark. I feel like I was definitely a spark that led to some positive change.'

He took those learnings even further. 'It kind of shows the need for public spaces,' he adds, 'and for us to be able to get together, because there's not too many places where you can go and just like exist for free.'

• • •

The rims, of course, are just part of this story, as Toronto artist Shane Stirling points out to me. He works at the intersection of sports, culture, music, and fashion, and has collaborated with Drake, among other ventures. 'Have you ever seen a baseball diamond where, on the pitcher's mound, there is a sewer grate?' he asks. 'Or have you ever seen a hockey rink with a sewer grate – where we've got Sidney Crosby skating down the ice, and his skate gets caught in the grate and he slips and breaks it? You ever seen a tennis court that is sunken down a foot and a half with a concrete curb, or one where there's no twenty-foot fence so the ball doesn't fly onto it?

'What I just described,' he continues, 'are three very identifiable features of the number one basketball court, outdoors, in Toronto.' Stirling is referring to a court in Toronto's Esplanade neighbourhood, a space that has been featured in numerous commercials presenting the city's commitment to basketball. That court, however, also features a sunken curb and concrete walls, with a sewer grate right at centre court.

'Have you ever been to an outdoor ice rink over in Bloor West Village, where you got these rinks and they all run with a little tuck shop and a change room for guys and girls?' he continues. 'It's nestled into the neighbourhood. It feels welcoming for an open skate, and you come with your girlfriend or your parents, then there's time for shinny and it engages the community. 'Have you ever seen that for basketball, with a washroom or changing room or drinking fountain or a tuck shop?'

No.

There's preferential treatment, arguably racist treatment, over how we plan our sports. Stirling agrees, somewhat. 'Well, look at all of our Toronto boys that are in the NHL currently, and I'm like, "Great, you would probably assume that there's more Toronto-born NHL players than Toronto-born NBA players." There's not. So what the fuck? Your point of reference, or what you know, is not necessarily insidious or evil or truly venomous racism. But there's a great lack of understanding of the way our city truly is.'

Stirling has plenty of engagement with basketball. His son competes at Orangeville Prep and is aiming to play collegiate ball. Consequently, he has more than a passing knowledge of the minutiae of the sport. 'Do you happen to know the dimensions – the regulation dimensions – of a basketball court?' he asks me during our chat in early 2020. Honestly, I don't know the answer off the top of my head.

Stirling does: ninety-four feet by fifty feet. The rims are typically ten feet off the ground. Like most people who play neighbourhood ball in this city, I grew up on courts with warped surfaces and distorted dimensions. On some courts, the rims were higher than ten feet. On others, there were no backboards, just rims attached to exterior walls. Fast-break layups posed a test for making the basket without crashing into brick.

As Stirling pointedly says, here we are, in the country that invented basketball, in a city that has become a hotbed of basketball culture because of the 2019 championship, in a region that is

Harbourfront Community Centre, at the foot of Bathurst Street, plays host to some of the most vibrant streetball in the downtown Toronto core. (Courtesy of Yasin Osman)

sending hundreds of talented players to NCAA teams, and still the powers that be can't build a proper outdoor court.

He then offers up a pair of stats that I can't readily find myself: 135 and 75. The first refers to the number of outdoor courts run by the City of Toronto – Stirling took the count himself – that are readily accessible and regulation size.

As for the second number, 75 – that's the number of indoor courts in a city of almost 3 million people. 'How many,' he asks, 'do you think are readily accessible, and regulation size?'

I guess less than 10 per cent.

'It's zero,' he replies. 'There's zero courts.'

In fact, many public indoor courts – in community centres, public schools, and recreation facilities – have not been updated to international basketball standards. But some, as with my nearby gym at Masaryk-Cowan, do get a new coat of paint.

Stirling and I really wrestle with something here. Basketball has never been so popular – socially, economically, even politically. Yet many gyms and courts are barely adequate and out of date. Would we tolerate this kind of neglect in hockey?

'Where's the money going?' Stirling wonders. 'I don't know. When you go to these courts in [neighbourhoods like] Malvern and Falstaff, you realize, "Oh, you spent $40,000 on vinyl application." I know because I work with Nike on experiential marketing installations. You could put lipstick on a pig, but it's still a pig. All they did was put up owls' – Drake's clothing brand, OVO – 'everywhere to make the kids feel like it's cool.'

'But they didn't actually fix the fact that the court at Falstaff, in [north Toronto neighbourhood] Willowdale, is ten feet too short, and the ceiling is so low that you can't shoot threes because you'd hit the rafters,' he adds. 'I know because I grew up playing hoops there – as did my son. It's so small that you can't even sit on a bench on the sideline – like it's actually a fire code issue.'

Like Luke Galati, Sterling wants to correct these disconnects and press the city to build properly sized courts, just the way it does with other sports infrastructure. As he points out, the absence of high-quality facilities not only tells a troubling story, it also leaves Toronto kids at a disadvantage.

Another one. And no one wants that.

6

BHATIA, DRAKE, AND THE MAKING
OF BASKETBALL CULTURE
IN THE 6IX

During the Raptors' historic 2019 playoff run, a car dealer from Mississauga, well-known to stalwart fans, became something of a global phenomenon. Ever since the team's first season in 1995, Nav Bhatia had attended every home game; for many years, he was a familiar presence to diehard Toronto fans as he sat near courtside, sporting vintage Raptors gear and cheering his head off.

His story is one of those archetypal immigrant tales. He fled India and anti-Sikh rioting in the mid-1980s. Unable to pursue his chosen profession – engineering – he started a new career: selling cars. Bhatia, it turned out, had the knack and broke all sorts of sales records, eventually moving up to own his own dealership, a Hyundai outlet that's become one of the busiest in Canada. Unflaggingly upbeat, he's been a recipient of the Top 25 Immigrant Entrepreneurs award and many other civic honours.

Along the way, he has given to charity, set up a foundation, promoted immigrant stories, and cheered for the Raptors so long and so enthusiastically that he came to be dubbed the team's 'superfan' – an honour that got him inducted into the Naismith Memorial Basketball Hall of Fame (the first fan to be so honoured). During the Raps' championship drive, the international media picked up his story. The team gave him a championship ring when they won, a first.

But if Bhatia put a face to Raptormania, another local celebrity, Drake, gave it a sound and a brand, and then showed the city how this sport tapped into the civic bloodstream of a region where so many young people, whose families came from all over the world and all walks of life, saw basketball as an entry point and a means of connecting. After all, basketball has become a cultural force because it's brought to the fore those parts of the city that were not heard or spoken of in a larger context. The sport's culture is, in part, the culture of newcomers, marginalized communities, and people of colour.

Some folks even argue that the sport is just straight-up Black culture. As Dan Klores, writing for *The Undefeated*, commented:

> Basketball, a game invented by a Canadian teaching in America, was first embraced by turn-of-the-century immigrants who settled in Northeastern port cities, then adopted as part of the national experience: by Southern blacks migrating North, company towns, church leagues, YMCAS, settlement homes, barnstorming clubs of men and women. It was and remains revered for its simplicity, escape and balletic free-form nature, as well as by its lessons of teamwork, discipline and sacrifice. It brought pride to the struggling individual, the group seeking to assimilate – and the community.

• • •

Drake, the world's top hip-hop recording artist, is the other face of basketball in Toronto. He's frequently courtside at Raptors games, trashtalking the opposing team. He has a popular clothing brand and ran a club in the city for a while, but is perhaps best known for branding Toronto as 'The 6ix,' a label that quickly replaced 'T-Dot' and 'Hogtown' as a regularly used civic nickname.

Born Aubrey Drake Graham, Drake, in the early 2000s, was a young guy coming off his acting work on *Degrassi: The Next*

Generation. He began to record, and put out a couple of singles, 'City Is Mine' and 'Do What You Do,' which were both produced by his long-time friend and collaborator Boi-1da. His singles were typical hip-hop tropes, but they didn't really say anything that would translate into something bigger and bolder.

And then Drake met Shane Stirling (see Chapter 5) – a Parkdale kid who grew up playing baseball and basketball and running track. But Stirling was also into visual arts – he was a doodler, a sketcher, and open-minded about other forms of visual expression. In his world, art spoke to sports and sports informed art – an intersection his buddies didn't get.

'All of my basketball friends would be like, "Hey, man, so are you gay?" That's a pretty intense question for the locker room when you're twelve years old, so I'm like, "Nah, but my boyfriend is," Stirling recalls, jokingly. 'Then I'm in my art class and I'm wearing a pair of Jordans and a city hat and they're like, "You're a weirdo." I'm like, "Why?" And they're like, "You like sports." I'm like, "Huh?! How is it weird that I like sports?" "Well, cuz you know, you're not following the stereotype of what an artist is." And I'm not following a stereotype of what an athlete is. So I was always kind of othered.'

Stirling also had a deep passion for hip hop from a young age. He grew up at a time when basketball was buried on the nightly sports highlight shows on TSN – coincidentally, *RapCity* on Much-Music television was buried on the evening channel schedule at 10:30 p.m. on Friday nights.

'I grew up with a deep appreciation for Master T, who presented a person like Bogle to the entire nation – where you have Bogle on television on a Saturday, explaining how to wine and do all the different dances which he created, as if he was Mr. Rogers,' Stirling says, referring to the late artist considered a pioneer in modern dancehall. 'Master T would come in, change his cardigan, put on his sneakers and present hip hop, and West Indian culture weekly.' It was, he recalls, inclusive, not exclusive. 'It was like, "This is culture, enjoy."'

Early in his career making videos, Stirling, like many others, found he had to work extrahard to advocate for hip hop in Canadian music. Many looked at the genre as being just 'a U.S. perspective,' not really understanding the penetrating, incisive impact that the art form was having on communities in the GTA. Through those gigs, he was introduced to Drake: 'I directed his first music video and was responsible for getting him on *106 & Park* with an independent video – that is, an *independent* Canadian video of a half-white, half-Black, Jewish kid right from an affluent part of Toronto.' They were kindred spirits – both very artsy, with a deep interest in bringing hip hop into a new sphere. Stirling had a vision of where he wanted to take his new collaborator: 'When I met Drake, I said to him, "Hey, I'm going to make you an emblem of aspirational living."'

But, he added, 'it needs to be about global aspirations.' Drake asked Shane what he meant. 'I'm like, "Well, you have to be the person that jumps on the plane with just the Louis duffle." And he goes, "What's a Louis duffle?"'

Stirling put Drake in touch with the late Chris Lighty, a music industry legend who discovered 50 Cent, Busta Rhymes, LL Cool J, and Missy Elliott. They'd been working together to scout talent north of the border, and Stirling had seen something in Drake.

The song Stirling directed, 'Replacement Girl,' premiered on April 30, 2007, on BET's flagship music program, with Trey Songz singing the chorus. It was a huge moment for Canadian hip hop. Canadian singles had performed on BET before, featuring rappers like Kardinal Offishall, Choclair, and k-os. Knowing this, Stirling pushed for 'Replacement Girl'; the rest, as they say, is history.

At roughly the same time, the Raptors were breaking new ground as a team, evolving from being a perennial also-ran in the NBA to a genuine contender. Drawing on his ideas about the relationship between sports and art, Stirling wanted to help basketball culture be heard. He had worked for Nike, including the iconic marketing and branding work on *Nike Battlegrounds*, for which he wrote all the copy in the 2000s.

After Drake got an endorsement deal with the Jordan brand in the early 2010s, Stirling heard rumblings it might be possible to get Drake a sponsorship deal with the Raptors. A Toronto professional sports franchise sponsoring a rapper – think about that for a moment. 'What was different about Drake more than anyone else I was working with at that point in time is that he listened,' Stirling says. 'He knew that great advice from a coach or a business partner or a creative is just words unless you apply them. That was his greatness.'

The Raptors, however, had not yet achieved greatness, at least not consistently. They were progressing in fits and starts, and had runs of bad luck in first rounds of the NBA playoffs. As a team, their popularity wasn't really penetrating much beyond its core constituencies. Stirling was dismayed. 'No kids are outside playing on courts,' he says. In fact, Drake early on hinted at his boredom. 'This one time, Drake pulls out a lint brush at the game, and Nike has agreed to do this [branding] concept. I'm like, "This is not good." Then the internet came for Drake because they don't like light-skinned kids from Canada running job – every little thing that he does wrong. "Now's the opportunity to end this. We need a guy from Brooklyn to take the reins, right?" And I said, "No, I'm not gonna let this happen."'

Stirling decided to ride the wave. In quick succession in 2014, Raptors president Masai Ujiri made a rant quickly dubbed 'Fuck Brooklyn.' Drake then slagged Jay-Z on social media for eating fondue. Stirling hustled up a triptych for Instagram and seeded it with influencers. The three graphics – Brooklyn, fondue, and a lint brush – all had red lines through them. Drake posted it. 'That shit,' Stirling says, 'went viral.'

Soon after, Drake's record and apparel company, October's Very Own (OVO), entered into a business partnership with the Raptors to 'ignite the culture of our game, in our city,' according to the official statement. (That partnership continues today, in smaller ways.)

The year after the triptych went wild, Stirling was approached by the City of Toronto to help animate a youth basketball event at the Mattamy Athletic Centre. Right off the bat, he was miffed. The Mattamy Athletic Centre? City officials were adamant about calling the space by its new corporate name. For Stirling and countless others, it's still Maple Leaf Gardens, a place of great sports history in this city – home of the Maple Leafs, the site of great WWF wrestling events, circus shows, and rock concerts. As an excited, rambunctious six-year-old, I met pro wrestling Hall of Famer the Undertaker on the floor of that arena during a house event. MLG's reinvention, complete with branding supplied by a suburban home builder, didn't have that spirit.

'In that moment, I realized we were talking a different language,' he says. Stirling wanted to help young basketballers have a voice as they continued their amateur and professional journeys. And he wanted that voice to carry.

He put together a decent campaign, but the city wasn't on board with a lot of his ideas. What he learned, however, served to motivate him to activate another marketing idea. 'When they decided to go in a different direction, I approached Nike and said, "Hey, I think I've tapped into what the culture needs right now. And I think it actually needs to go younger,"' he says. 'And I think that too often, culturally, we speak to an aged demographic. I was worried that music and basketball would go the way of Eaton's and Simpsons and Robinson's – all these Canadian institutions that just disappeared because they just got caught up marketing to an aging crowd.'

His focus fell elsewhere on the demographic spectrum: 'My opportunity to get to know these kids was easy because I'm also walking into every gym with the coolest gear, the hottest kicks – all this stuff. My access to their brains, their hearts, and their emotions was locked in because kids are smart. They read you from the shoes up. If you walk into a room and you're not that dude, they're gonna say, "You're not that dude, I don't care what your resumé says."'

After several months of recruiting, Stirling brought together a small cadre of amateur ballers, sixteen of them, in advance of the 2016 NBA All-Star Game in Toronto. The initial idea was that these kids, mostly boys at first, would tell their stories of playing the game. The small group also had a name: Vanguard Toronto. One of the more notable youth in that initial group was Nickeil Alexander-Walker, a now NBA player who had honed his basketball in Vaughan.

'6ixteen of the 6ix's finest have been selected for their unwavering passion for art, ball and culture,' Vanguard's website said. 'These young men possess an awareness and understanding that commentary isn't a commitment. They propel culture forward because they know observation isn't action. These boys put in that work, oh yeah you gonna learn today. These 16 young men from all ends of The 6ix are set to connect as storytellers to share, radiate and reflect on the art and culture of basketball.'

The group convened at the NIKEiD Studio in downtown Toronto for a chance to learn about the players' inspiration and explore their signature footwear. The Nike team then walked them through the footwear designs of Kobe Bryant, LeBron James, Kevin Durant, and Kyrie Irving, connecting the dots on how stories link to the apparel and the training the players undertake. It was very smart, clever work with kids who have so much promise.

By then, the association between Drake, the 6ix, and the Raptors had exploded into the region's consciousness – the business relationship between rapper and team continues. The cultural energy of basketball was expanding in so many ways. I think, for example, about the Hijabi Ballers' drop-in program – a non-profit celebrating and increasing opportunities for Muslim women in sports in the region. First organized by Torontonian Amreen Kadwa in 2017, the organization counters the discrimination that women face when they have chosen to don these articles of clothing.

'Hijab is not a preventative piece of cloth,' she told the *Toronto Star*. 'Women play any sport you can imagine from basketball to surfing to table tennis to soccer to beach volleyball to para-bocce ball. Wearing hijab is an extremely personal decision. And one that shouldn't affect an athlete's ability or right to partake in sport.'

The Hijabi Ballers project sees upwards of about 1,200 participants and attendees annually. (Courtesy of Yasin Osman)

Hijabi Ballers had been collaborating with the Muslim Women's Summer Basketball League, which is dedicated to bringing Muslim women in Toronto and the surrounding areas together through basketball. Fitriya Mohamed, who founded the league and serves as an ambassador for Hijabi Ballers, is clear in her intentions. Muslim women can practise their faith as they choose and also tear up the court. As she told the *Star*: 'It's truly just a matter of having space for us. The conversation has begun.'

7

COACHING AS IF YOUR LIFE
DEPENDED ON IT

For many Toronto sports fans, the line between the Raptors and their own lives goes past the television set or a computer that livestreams ESPN or TSN coverage. But for women like Lee Anna Osei, basketball has been so much more than something to watch or play casually. The sport has shaped her life, and she's using those lessons to shape the lives of others.

Osei grew up in the Jane and Finch neighbourhood, played for the Eastern Commerce girls' team, and was part of the squad that won OFSAA with head coach Kareem Griffin. Osei and Griffin go way back. 'He's literally like my brother,' she says. 'When I was in high school, I was homeless. Kareem was my coach for all four of my years at Eastern. When I really didn't have anywhere to go, he moved to downtown Toronto so that I could live at his place with his mom.'

That act of selflessness helped Osei navigate the real world with purpose. She became a student coach at Eastern and eventually acquired the credentials – on and off the court – to be scouted and recruited by American colleges, earning a spot at the University of Miami. She came back to Canada, completing a BA and then a master's degree from Wilfrid Laurier University in Waterloo. She now coaches the women's basketball team at St. Francis Xavier University in Antigonish, Nova Scotia.

Basketball has provided something far more special to Osei than just a profession. Through grassroots community events, like the annual Jane and Finch classic tournaments or free basketball camps, she's watched how a sense of competition grows among the people with whom she's played.

Is the competition healthy? She doesn't hesitate. 'It's created more opportunities and more platforms for students, for coaches, for jobs. I think if our grassroots level wasn't so sound – if there weren't too many people contributing to these young people – it would take away from a lot of success that we've recently had.'

The sense of competition extends from organized leagues to the school-based programs, and the choices for participating have multiplied in recent years. 'If you're a kid, there's so many options, but I don't think that was always the case,' says Osei. 'When I was coming up, the organizations were few and far between. Everybody wanted to play for the provincial team. They'd say, "Our priorities are going to the States or getting scholarships or, you know, getting better at coaching."'

When she came back to Canada and finished her degree at Laurier, Osei helped found Canletes Sports with Griffin. The organization aims to enhance the visibility of women in sport. 'We did things like highlight reels, publish game recaps, and tournament all-stars,' Osei recounts. She also helped program girls' basketball camps and alumni events for women players and coaches.

'We offered recruitment, consulting, and training. And that's when I really started to work with a lot of our guys, and a lot of our girls [in high school environments]. It's been a mixture of skill development training and kind of putting on basketball events.'

Griffin had his own take on Canletes and the space that gender occupies in this sport. 'Women's basketball, women's sports, are fun,' Griffin said in an interview. 'Because it's not driven by money, you see the purities of sport. You see the toughness, you see the players going after it because they're really going after it. In women's basketball, they don't take anything for granted because they're not given anything to begin with. Everything that they get, they appreciate.'

Yet, from her position in coaching, and with her own history, Osei wondered what kind of support was available to coaches in

Nova Scotia who were Black or Indigenous, or other people of colour. What she found is that supports are inadequate. 'We see that with African Nova Scotians, there's an endowment that is given to schools in the Maritimes – so across these seven institutions here – and it's a couple of thousand bucks just meant to help you,' she says. 'If you're not in a position where you have money – you're kind of in this big pool of maybe applying for some need-based grants that are like a shot in the dark.' But it's not enough.

● ● ●

As Osei knew from her own frustrating experiences in accessing support, a significant gender gap exists in Canadian inter-university sport and leadership positions, such as coaching and administration. According to a 2020 academic study published in the *International Journal of Sport Policy and Politics*, co-authored by University of Toronto professors Peter Donnelly and Bruce Kidd, in collaboration with McMaster's Mark Norman, men comprised 56 to 58 per cent of student athletes in Canada between 2011 and 2016–2017. As for coaching and administrative leadership positions, the study found that men accounted for 81 to 84 per cent of head coaches, and 78 to 80 per cent of assistant coaches. Men also made up 76 to 83 per cent of directors of athletics and 42 to 60 per cent of assistant directors of athletics.

Many coaches are underpaid. But besides the gender and pay gap, there's an even wider racial one. Osei was the first Black woman coach to serve at her university, and the experience of breaking barriers has been less than smooth. During her inaugural 2018–19 basketball season, she was suspended over an incident that occurred during a practice. Aside from a tough first season in charge of StFX, in 2018–19, the stories she heard from other coaches included accusations that the Black coaches were intimidating, uncaring, and even undeserving. She knew at least two other coaches of colour who she felt had been improperly dismissed.

That experience was a turning point and provided a moment of clarity. There were clear gaps for people of colour in that community – money, networking, all types of resources. Her conclusion was that BIPOC coaches across Canada needed a platform: a voice, a safe space, and support.

Taking inspiration from the National Association of Basketball Coaches and Canada's Black Business and Professional Association, she pulled together people from her networks and established the Black Canadian Coaches Association (BCCA). Its goal was to create equity-seeking campaigns to create a better future for equity-seeking groups – Black and Indigenous communities, and other people of colour, within Canadian post-secondary institutions.

'We come together once a year and celebrate the contributions of all these amazing people that are contributing to our sports sector,' says Osei. 'So that we have a reason to bring our Olympians and our NBA players and anybody else to speak to our youth so that our corporate sector and public sector or private sector partners can say, "Oh, look, there's a pool of people graduating that we can employ. We can intentionally go after these diverse individuals."'

One of the BCCA's first efforts was the creation of the Charter for Racial Equity in Canadian Postsecondary Institutions, which gave rise to the Racial Equity Project, a study aimed at collecting race-based data outlining the experience of Black and Indigenous people of colour in coaching. The BCCA wanted to take an evidence-informed approach to eradicating systemic racism by collecting anecdotal and statistical data that sought to validate experiences, raise awareness, and provide anti-racism education.

The project has numerous calls to action, including the appointment of equity committees for major post-secondary sports organizations nationwide, anti-racism and anti-discrimination training programs, advocacy for diversity in hiring committees, supports for racialized sports leaders, and creating means for financial assistance.

The BCCA's work aligns with the BlackNorth Initiative, which was established in Toronto by the Canadian Council of Business

Leaders Against Anti-Black Systemic Racism. It is composed of three hundred business leaders from across the country.

'We're trying to make history here and advocating for the Charter for Racial Equity and post-secondary athletics, something that is long overdue,' Osei says. 'We think it's practical, it's feasible. It provides us a baseline with how we start to renegotiate these spaces to make them more inclusive – more safe, mentally and physically.'

The BCCA launched in the summer of 2020, with the goal of introducing the broader coaching community to the organization and laying out its plans to begin planting seeds for future action and advocacy. Many coaches, including those from Concordia, Brock, and McMaster universities, spoke up in support of the BCCA. Dozens more asked how they could help and what the next steps were. There were also white coaches on the call, tuning in to show their solidarity.

To date, the group's calls to action have been taken up by twelve institutions across the country, including St. Francis Xavier, U of T Mississauga, and Brandon University in Manitoba. That list will continue to grow over time as the BCCA's presence spreads – a testament to the fact that the combined energies of one young woman of colour and her deeply empathetic basketball coach can – and will – alter the lives of so many other kids who are drawn to the courts, not just in Toronto but across the country.

8

CHILDREN AT THE VANGUARD

Across the region, basketball has become a home for something that goes beyond the game itself, and you can see that progress in the faces of children.

Sakina, a young girl about eight years old, wearing white ball shoes and matching grey hijab and T-shirt, grins brightly in the courtyard of her apartment building in Flemingdon Park, a high-rise neighbourhood located along the Don Valley in the old borough of North York. She's posing in front of the bright white balconies of the apartment building where she lives with her family.

In another photo, Sakina stands with her brothers, Musab and Yahya, in front of Thorncliffe Park Public School, under a basketball backboard with its rim removed. In a stop motion–like GIF, the trio goof around in some frames and stand proud and happy in others.

These images are the work of photographer Ebti Nabag, who recorded with the young baller in the summer of 2020. During a pandemic that hit these high-rise communities with particular ferocity, she was participating in Lay-Up, a program established in 2013 to provide cost-free hoops to kids from all corners of the city. The organization's program director, Chris Penrose, had recruited Nabag to create a virtual exhibit. She is a Ryerson University MFA grad who tells stories of 'often neglected' people and uses her work to connect with her home country, Sudan, and its people and culture. The result was the *At Home, in the Game* virtual exhibition.

'Lay-Up is a great way to get active at home, and it's entertaining and gives you lots of things to do. It was perfect,' Sakina told Nabag. 'I didn't know the drills, and that helped me to get better in skills.'

'What was one thing that you liked most about your coaches?' Nabag asked.

'I liked how supportive and kind they were,' Sakina replied. 'I had an entertaining summer and all the activities were amazing.'

Of all the children Nabag photographed and interviewed for the project, Sakina was her favourite. 'She was shy at the beginning,' Nabag tells me. 'She had two other brothers with her in the program. As we were taking photos, and I had them really, like, jump and interact and just be silly and goofy, and help out with holding a reflector and things like that, she really loosened up. By the end, she was engaging.'

• • •

Free basketball programs for kids and youth haven't always had such a positive profile. Penrose says many were cringeworthy in a lot of ways: kids weren't really learning skills, staff weren't really coaching. Just kids 'running around the gym,' he says. Then there was midnight basketball, which city officials in Toronto and elsewhere figured was some kind of anti-gang gesture.

So when Penrose joined Lay-Up in 2019, he arrived with a vision. 'I had this idea: how do you take the structure and the growth opportunities in elite basketball development camps and provide that cost-free?' Then he saw something else germinate: 'How do you create a great experience in basketball for kids who aren't trying to go anywhere in basketball? Or maybe it's their second or third or fourth or fifth favourite sport.'

One thing Penrose was looking to accomplish when he joined was making sure that Lay-Up wasn't stereotyping the participants or the neighbourhoods where the program operated using a 'deficit language.' He knew that in the non-profit sector, fundraisers

Sakina (R), Musab (L), and Yahya, three siblings, took part in the At Home, In the Game *virtual multimedia exhibit, shot by Toronto-based portrait and documentary photographer Ebti Nabag. (Courtesy of Ebti Nabag)*

use sad stories to entice philanthropists. 'We were just, like, we don't want to ever describe the user communities in a way that they themselves wouldn't be proud of,' he says.

Sure, he wanted to draw attention to inequities. But for Penrose, the important goal was not to make the participants and their communities the problem. They are the solution. 'There are so many stories of community and collaboration and resilience and innovation and ingenuity that are happening despite systemic racism and barriers.'

Lay-Up provided quality camps and activities until the coronavirus pandemic closed the program's doors temporarily in the communities that Lay-Up serves: Toronto's thirty-one Neighbourhood Improvement Areas, a euphemistic label that provides the backbone for the city's strong neighbourhoods strategy. Penrose's team pivoted to providing a variety of online workshops aimed at physical activity, creativity, and maintaining meaningful connections. About three hundred kids from Jane and Finch, Malvern, Thorncliffe Park, Regent Park, Rexdale, Mount Dennis, Woburn, and Kingston/Galloway took part.

Sakina, Musab, and Yahya were photographed and interviewed at Thorncliffe Park Public School. (Courtesy of Ebti Nabag)

This is where Nabag comes in. For her project on Lay-Up, she connected with twelve kids in their communities to create a collage of images of young people as they navigated the pandemic in their neighbourhoods. Each has a story to tell. One little boy, Emijah, is soaking it all in as he stands tall with a basketball under his foot on a sidewalk in Malvern, a neighbourhood in the former borough of Scarborough. Sarah, outside of her Flemingdon apartment building, is rocking red-and-white high-tops and standing with confidence with a basketball. Emmanuel, on a blacktop in the Jane and Finch area, is posing as if he's waiting for the ball to post up.

The vision behind the exhibit, Nabag explained, speaks to her deep belief that basketball has become so much more than a game. 'I remember having a conversation with a friend regarding Kobe's accident,' she tells me, in a chat after the launch. (Kobe Bryant died in a helicopter crash in January 2020, with his daughter and several other parents and children who were all members of the same girls' basketball team.) 'It was about how much he was praised and how many people came out [to his memorial] and the overwhelming emotions everyone was experiencing.'

Her friend shrugged at the tributes: 'He's just a basketball player.' Nabag was furious. It's more than basketball. It's a ticket for a lot of people; it builds leadership and gives you so many transferrable skills that don't just remain within the realm of sports. I think that's what I learned from Lay-Up – that basketball is an avenue, a tiny piece of this larger opportunity. It's never just basketball.

Penrose echoes these sentiments: 'I think, for me, basketball is really special because every sport faces challenges in terms of being accessible and being inclusive. But I think basketball is among one of the more accessible and inclusive sports. You don't need a ton of infrastructure to play the game. Even innovations like wheelchair basketball increase the accessibility.' He feels there's still plenty more runway. 'I think there's a lot of potential to make it even more inclusive, and even more accessible.'

In his view, and probably those of the kids who come through Lay-Up, basketball should be the 'official sport of Toronto.' Maybe it already is. Does that mean Toronto is now truly a haven of equity, inclusivity, and accessibility? No. But perhaps we're farther along that road than we think we are.

9
KEEPING YOUR EYE ON THE BALL

Once upon a time, in a hockey rink not so far away, a game was being hotly contested. The rink is known as Century Gardens. Have you ever been? Located on Vodden Street East, in Brampton, the Gardens is a massive site with two ice rinks, a swimming pool, a fitness centre, and an auditorium. Architecturally, the building is very much in that twenty-first-century suburban style, and it literally houses gardens.

Like Vaughan, Brampton has been rapidly changing for decades. Forget the influx of people or the increased traffic and suburbanization. Just look at what is physically there. A lot of Brampton was farmland until the 1990s. Open fields sold off by farmers who couldn't push back against the changing times.

As for recreation and active living, the great urbanization of Brampton meant that the city built it and they came. Promoted by former Brampton mayor Susan Fennell, the 'Making Great Things Happen' initiative delivered two new community centres and two renovated and expanded recreation centres as part of a $120 million capital program in 2008. In June 2007, the Brampton Soccer Centre at Dixie Road and Sandalwood Parkway opened to much fanfare. Later that same summer, Earnscliffe Recreation Centre on Eastbourne Drive reopened following an expansion and extensive renovations. The Cassie Campbell Community Centre at Sandalwood Parkway and Chinguacousy opened in fall 2008, honouring one of the stars of Canadian women's hockey.

Fennell is a deeply interesting person, and her name sparks two significant story streams that I have followed. She was highly involved in women's hockey, most notably as the founder and first commissioner of the National Women's Hockey League, and she founded a local club, the Brampton Thunder, which existed from 1999 to 2006. According to a 2005 profile in the *Globe and Mail*:

> By her own account, brassy Brampton Mayor Susan Fennell has become the matron saint of women's hockey. A classic sports promoter, she whipped a ragtag collection of enthusiasts in mismatched uniforms into an expansion-minded amateur league. She spends two hours a day – midnight to 2:00 a.m. – firing off email messages to her hockey network. She talks to National Hockey League commissioner Gary Bettman about joint projects. And she harangued Governor-General Adrienne Clarkson into sponsoring a championship trophy, in the tradition of Lord Stanley.

The NWHL was the precursor to the Canadian Women's Hockey League, which was prominent for much of the 2010s. The CWHL featured the likes of Sami Jo Small, the backup goalie for the 2002 and 2006 Olympic women's hockey teams; Tessa Bonhomme, who went on to work in hockey broadcasting; and Meghan Agosta, the MVP of the women's 2010 Olympic Games tournament in Vancouver.

The CWHL was elite, but unfortunately it didn't have the kind of financial support that serves the NHL and other men's pro leagues worldwide. Many of the players continue to play for club and country – including for a newer iteration of the NWHL called the Premier Hockey Federation. That league fields only one Canadian club, the Toronto Six. The play is some of the most incredible competition I've ever seen in women's hockey.

Fennell worked closely with Hazel McCallion, her former mayoral counterpart in Mississauga, on the business of women's hockey. The two should be lauded for their contributions to the game. This is the story by which I prefer to think of Fennell.

The other narrative is less edifying. Fennell was caught up in several corruption scandals as mayor. Most famously, as reported by the *Toronto Star*, she was accused of secretly and illegally lowering her own salary in 2013 to avoid the publicity of being the highest-paid mayor in Canada. She also racked up numerous spending scandals, including a $50,000 bill for airfare expenses while in office. She defended herself by saying the expenses complied with council policy.

A local developer, Inzola Group Limited, sued Fennell in 2011, accusing her and members of her former staff of bias and political interference in Mississauga's $500 million Southwest Quadrant Renewal project procurement process in 2009. That lawsuit was later dismissed.

Even while these controversies were swirling, she was aggressively building and expanding Brampton, proposing more dense neighbourhoods and approving the construction of a wide variety of sports facilities.

So when Fennell finally christened the newly renovated Century Gardens, she was more than happy to flag its benefits for the community. 'The renovation and expansion of Century Gardens is part of a City-wide initiative to provide high-quality and responsive recreation facilities and programs to everyone in Brampton,' Fennell said in an official statement. 'This is part of the City's focus on creating healthy and active lifestyle opportunities for people of all ages.'

What distinguishes this particular venue is that it adds space for organized sports that take place on large municipal rink complexes. Indeed, Century Gardens is perhaps best known around Brampton as the venue for one of the region's largest and most anticipated ball-hockey tournaments – an annual event called the Khalsa Cup, which features teams whose athletes are mostly Canadians of Sikh descent.

In many predominantly South Asian neighbourhoods in Peel Region, which includes Mississauga and Brampton, hockey is a consuming passion. The Punjabi broadcast of *Hockey Night in Canada*, which started in 2011, draws tens of thousands of viewers. Local efforts to introduce ice hockey to South Asian kids have sprung up in recent years. There's even a movie on the subject: *Breakaway*. A 2011 Canadian sports comedy, it tells the story of Rajvinder, a Hindi Punjabi-Canadian player who struggles against traditional family values and discrimination from mainstream hockey players. It has sports, romance, and an exploration of Rajvinder's obsession with a game that doesn't exactly love him back.

The charitable proceeds earned from the Khalsa Cup ball hockey tournament goes to a different charitable cause every year. (Courtesy of Hockey 4 Humanity)

The Khalsa Cup is a ball-hockey tournament with a loyal following – hundreds have taken part. In its first year, a three-day event in 2014 at Huron Park Arena in Mississauga, there were 180 players on twelve teams. That number grew to about 200 in the 2019 tourney. In 2014, the tournament raised about $6,000 for the Khalra Centre for Human Rights Defenders, which is based in Delhi. They have since raised tens of thousands of dollars more.

The event, a fundraiser collaboratively organized by the Sikh Youth Federation, the Champions Ball Hockey League, Toronto Singh's Camp, and the World Sikh Organization of Canada, is well attended. Unlike most sports fundraisers, the Khalsa Cup incorporates the Sikh concepts of *seva* and *sarbat da bhalla*. *Seva* in Sanskrit refers to selfless service; *sarbat da bhalla* refers to blessings for everyone, a Sikh prayer that all will prosper. 'That was very intentionally designed into the tournament so it's not just any other event,' says Jaskaran Singh Sandhu, a lawyer, campaign strategist, and one of the fundraiser's organizers. 'There's a very specific goal here beyond just the sport.'

He explains it to me: 'How do you continue to build those events around everything you do? And how do you encourage young kids to start thinking like that about every action they take in their life, that higher living is not siloed off when you go to the gurdwaras or when you go to the mosque or your church or what-ever it is on the weekend. It's supposed to be a philosophy that you fill into everything you do.'

Events like the Khalsa Cup fit neatly into his world view. 'Sport is like this equalizer of sorts, a common platform where everyone can come hang out and talk. It becomes this meeting place where folks that otherwise would never engage with one another engage with one another and expand networks … and that strengthens the community in multiple ways.'

In the run-up to the 2019 cup, the players engaged in some healthy trash talk while expressing a deep appreciation for the moment at Century Gardens. Before the first match, Harjaap Singh, a local host for the Sikh Channel, spoke to the captain of the Khalsa Snipers, a tight-knit ball-hockey team based in Brampton.

'So what we're hearing is that the Khalsa Snipers are pretty favoured for this competition. They have a great history,' he said.

'They suck!' chirped an opposing player from the Brampton Predators.

'So we have a lot of healthy criticism, as well!' Harjaap replied.

Harjaap got back on track and asked the captain of the Snipers, Amritpal Kooner, about the team, its history, and their goal for the final. 'The team was started about fifteen years ago, and that was the original Khalsa Snipers team,' the captain replied. 'They played together for years and years. And when we were all little kids – around maybe twelve, thirteen – we started playing together at the Powerade Centre.

'The older Khalsa Snipers guys would coach us, they would come to practise with us, and every day we'd be praying, practising, and slowly more people would be joining our team.'

This club was a family and still is. 'I've been playing with everyone since I was in Grade 9, and since then our team has grown to about twenty-five guys,' says Kooner. 'It's honestly become like a family – that's what we do. We like to play hockey; we like to hang out.'

But Sandhu points out that the appeal is rooted in the complexities and limitations of the immigrant experience. 'These are second- and third-generation guys who grew up loving hockey, from immigrant families that can't necessarily afford to take the kids to ice hockey. The criticism of ice hockey is that it lacks diversity, it is not a place that new immigrants and new Canadians find welcoming.'

'Ball hockey,' he continues, 'is the opposite. Some of the best players in competitive ball hockey in the world are actually Brown kids from Brampton. And it's absolutely wild because while the folks in ice hockey are kind of scratching their heads on how to get people engaged, ball hockey is home to such crazy diversity that is just not seen anywhere else.'

• • •

There's a stark irony that ball hockey has become such a huge draw among South Asians *because* of the barriers to playing ice hockey in a region that brags about its diversity. Lauded by politicians and the media, hockey is placed on a pedestal as part of our nation-building narrative. Its advocates not only want Canadians to be the best players in the world, they think all Canadians should be playing it regularly, and with abandon. Greater Toronto, in particular, is home to the world's largest amateur hockey league (the Greater Toronto Hockey League) and continues to produce some of the world's best players.

As the *Toronto Star*'s Sean Fitz-Gerald, who wrote a book about the changing landscape of hockey in the GTA, points out, Canadians participate in a wide range of physical activities, from swimming to ballet, but 'we only put one of these sports on the back of our money.' The symbolism, however, no longer aligns with the reality, especially in a region as diverse as the GTA. As Fitz-Gerald says, hockey 'is expensive and it's not fun anymore. Kids are dropping out faster than they're signing up.'

Money is a big part of the problem. A 2019 survey conducted by Scotiabank and FlipGive, a team-funding app, found that 60 per cent of Canadian hockey parents spend more than $5,000 each year on equip-

The Khalsa Cup has implemented the concepts of seva *(selfless service in Sanskrit)* and sarbat da bhalla *(may good come to all)* into the highly competitive ball hockey play. *(Courtesy of Hockey 4 Humanity)*

ment, training, rink fees, league fees, and specialized nutrition. Based on interviews with a thousand American and Canadian parents, the survey also found about one in four Canadian hockey parents take on another job to fund the season.

In fact, a 2013 study conducted by the Canadian Council for Refugees found that many immigrants, newcomers, and refugees begin their Canadian experiences in serious debt (to the tune of thousands of dollars – and more, in some cases), which means that enrolling themselves or their kids in organized hockey is not an option, much less a priority.

Consequently, demand in many neighbourhoods is going down. In 2017, a City of Toronto report forecast recreational needs out to the late 2030s and made recommendations on how municipal resources should be invested. A key conclusion that many people found startling: Toronto has too many ice rinks and many of them are becoming obsolete. The city's challenge is figuring out how to adjust to changing times.

Gender offers another wrinkle. For organized girls' and women's hockey, demand is rising, but venues remain hard to come by, and cost is also an impediment. The Leaside Wildcats, a talented girls' team, has a roster of families that can afford equipment, rink fees, training sessions, and inter-city tournaments. But they're the exception, not the rule.

Then there's the racism that Sandhu and so many others have encountered. In the GTHL, stories of explicit and implicit incidents of discrimination abound. In one report by CTV News in June 2020, several youth players, including sixteen-year-old Myles Douglas from Georgetown, Ontario, said that they were routinely targeted with verbal and racialized insults. 'I'd probably say, like, half of the games someone said something, but no one ever heard,' Myles told CTV News. 'They always say it when the refs' backs are turned, or when they know the refs or no one else will hear them.'

To create the Toronto we want, and even the sports environment we want, we need to become more equitable in our planning. Right now, we're moving too slowly. The consequences for downplaying systemic, subtle, and deliberate forms of racism and discrimination in hockey have driven some people away entirely.

The Khalsa Snipers won the 2019 Khalsa Cup tournament – an overtime win over the Brampton Predators. (Courtesy of Hockey 4 Humanity)

10
HARRY GAIREY'S ENDURING LESSON

Long before South Asian ball-hockey players made their presence felt on Brampton's rinks, a Jamaican-born Canadian who worked on the railroads in his youth took it upon himself to banish the casual institutional racism that defined who could and could not play shinny on Toronto rinks.

In the 1940s and 1950s, Harry Gairey Sr. worked as a railway porter, a common job for Black men in Canada in the early twentieth century. Black people who had immigrated here from Caribbean nations were removed from everyday life in Toronto. This was not a northern version of Jim Crow; rather, it was a form of segregation that forced Black men to leave their families to work in an office that shunted them all over Canada.

Gairey lived a porter's life, which meant harsh working conditions and a lack of promotions into other railway jobs. But he pushed back in the 1950s, helping to form the Brotherhood of Sleeping Car Porters of Canada, which was instrumental in pressing the federal government to legislate fair labour practices. Gairey, with the Negro Citizenship Association, also lobbied Ottawa for changes to immigration laws.

In addition to his activism, we need to pay attention to Gairey's experiences with sports in Toronto. In 1945, his son, Harry Jr., was barred from skating on the Icelandia rink in midtown Toronto. The reason? The child was Black. 'While his white companions were allowed into Icelandia,' local history writer Jamie Bradburn writes on his history blog, 'Gairey Jr. was notified by rink manager Bedford Allen that "no coloured boys can come in here." Harry's friends saw what happened, turned around, and asked for a refund.'

Gairey stood up for his boy. He arranged to appear before the Board of Control, which was the executive committee of Toronto's city council.

'With tears in his eyes,' Bradburn recounts, 'Gairey Sr. offered apologies for taking the council's time, to which Mayor Robert Saunders replied, "I don't know that we have anything more valuable on which to spend our time than looking into a matter like this."'

Quoting *A Black Man's Toronto, 1914–1980: The Reminiscences of Harry Gairey*, Bradburn recounts what Gairey told city council: 'Now it would be all right if the powers that be refused my son admission to the Icelandia, I would accept it, if when the next war comes, you're going to say, "Harry Gairey, you're black, you stay here, don't go to war." But, your Worship, and Gentlemen of the Council, it's not going to be that way; you're going to say he's a Canadian and you'll conscript him. And, if so, I would like my son to have everything a Canadian citizen is entitled to, providing he's worthy of it.'

Despite protests at the rink and further incidents of discrimination at Icelandia, the city changed its policy. The right to use all spaces without enduring discrimination was enshrined, cementing Gairey's connection to Toronto skating rinks forever.

Gairey went on to establish the first Toronto community centre for Caribbean-born people in the city – in the Annex neighbourhood, on Brunswick Avenue. For many older Black people I know and love, this hub was right around the corner from their first apartments when they arrived in Canada. Shortly after Gairey died in 1993, the outdoor skating rink at Scadding Court Community Centre in nearby Alexandra Park was named in his honour. It's a go-to for outdoor skating to this day – a place that has sought to include marginalized communities in hockey for many years.

• • •

Gairey's spirit was evident on March 30, 2019, at the inaugural Roundtable on Racism in Hockey. The forum brought about fifty delegates to the Queen's University campus in Kingston to consider questions about racialized experiences in hockey. One key theme: why were communities of colour, like the many South Asian hockey enthusiasts living in Peel Region, so absent from the profile of mainstream hockey in Canada?

One of the attendees was Lali Toor, who grew up in Edmonton and ended up playing elite hockey as a teenager in British Columbia. He knew all about racism in hockey, which had reared its head early and often. 'The first time I really started feeling it was when I was at the age of ten,' he recounts. 'You notice that some parents wouldn't like you on your own team.' Opposing teams would yell obscenities and parents would yell over the boards, trying to knock him off his game. And coaches went out of their way to cut him from tryouts and teams. 'At one point,' he says, 'I was actually kicked out of an organization halfway through the season at the age of ten [for no reason].'

Eventually, he quit. 'I was sick and tired of it. I fell in love with the game at such a young age. I loved hockey, but hockey hurt me. It just seems that hockey never fully reciprocates the love that ethnic minorities have for it, right?'

The keynote speaker for the roundtable was Eugene Arcand, who is Cree from Treaty 6 territory and served as a member of the Truth and Reconciliation Commission (TRC) Indian Residential School Survivor Committee. A talented athlete in his youth, Arcand is known for his role in promoting sports, recreation, and cultural opportunities for First Nations youth in Saskatchewan — especially in Indigenous-organized hockey, which has long endured its own ugly confrontations with racism.

Arcand, a shy man, agreed to participate, but he had a condition he shared with one of the event's main organizers, Courtney Szto, who teaches at Queen's School of Kinesiology and Health Studies and researches the relationship between physical cultures and intersectional justice. 'He said, "I will come if

you guys make sure that this isn't just words that we're doing,'"
she recalls. 'He said we needed to create a policy paper – something
that was going to go to Hockey Canada specifically.'

Through her work, Szto has come to many conclusions about
the sport, one of which is that hockey culture is not monolithic.
'I think that that's what the media generally loves to hammer
down on,' she says. In a CBC interview, she was asked if hockey
culture is toxic. 'I was like, "Well, that's a leading question," because
aspects of it are certainly toxic, but other aspects are absolutely
wonderful. So I think it's important for people to realize that one
locker room's culture can be so different from another locker
room's culture, and they can be in the same room and they can
be in the same league.'

The discussion during the roundtable broadened her thinking
and produced the report Arcand had requested. Entitled 'Changing
on the Fly,' the document showed how discrimination and a lack
of diversity within hockey explained the lack of South Asian
participation. It was a landmark paper, and Szto later expanded
it into a book: *Changing on the Fly: Hockey through the Voices of South
Asian Canadians.*

Changing on the Fly was inspired by the TRC's calls to action on
sport, which helped form its policy recommendations. 'Our inspiration really was to help tailor those recommendations in a hockey
setting,' Szto says. 'The TRC is obviously more about Indigenous
equality, but it opens the doors for discussions about anti-racism
more broadly in Canada.'

They framed their recommendations around power, privilege,
and access, 'with the belief that that's how you create genuine
equality,' she says. 'And *power* was really around who's sitting at
the table and who has decision-making power.'

All of this was valiant and necessary work, but were the hockey
powers that be listening?

As it transpired, some hockey organizations did respond. The
GTHL, which had held its own summit on culture, inclusivity, and
diversity that same year, announced in 2020 that it would address

issues of racism and discrimination in minor hockey – including 'appointing an Independent Committee that will be asked to examine issues that are identified through the course of discussions,' according to an official statement.

One of the issues the league seeks to tackle is racial epithets. 'Recently, the GTHL has been asked about penalties assessed to GTHL players for racist comments,' the league stated, citing its 'strict zero tolerance policy.' 'A player receiving such a penalty is subject to an automatic indefinite suspension, pending a review process to determine the length of the suspension.'

But such accountability measures go only so far. While some critics say that offenders' identities should be made public, the GTHL has refused, citing school board and youth criminal justice policies: 'When considering whether to release any such information, we take into account the interests of all parties and all relevant factors. We are careful not to breach privacy obligations.' In other words, privacy will keep racist beliefs private and thus not confronted.

Lali Toor had other ideas – or maybe he wasn't prepared to wait for Canada's hockey establishment to get its act together. While he was preparing for his GMAT exam, he made friends with his professor – also a South Asian man – and they went to an Edmonton Oilers game together. 'I told him, like, kind of what happened with me,' Toor recalls, and he also shared an idea. He wanted to give young South Asian kids – boys and girls – more exposure to more competitive hockey leagues, including the major junior hockey and professional ranks. 'I wanted to do a hockey camp for them and make sure that they all knew one another,' he says, 'that they know there's other players that look like us.'

He even had a concept for what to call the program: Apna Hockey – *apna* means *our*. Toor's goal was nothing less than lifting up hockey players of colour all over Canada, including those in all those ball-hockey leagues in Peel Region. He also wanted to create a safe space where newcomer hockey parents can speak their own language and not feel afraid. It was an idea he had been sitting on since he'd quit playing.

His professor friend loved the plan and encouraged Toor to keep going. So he and his friends started doing some promotion and corralled a few sponsors to make sure kids under ten could take part for free. He asked other friends who played competitively to come in to provide instruction.

That first camp, held in Edmonton, was a big success, and Apna's operations expanded rapidly to other cities. 'Since April 2017, anything South Asian hockey-related just ran through our organization – or we're aware of it, or we help out other organizations that want to set up anything remotely.' Toor and Apna Hockey worked with the *Hockey Night in Canada* Punjabi team to help spread the word.

What they didn't need to do was sell young people on hockey itself. 'The love for the game is so, so deeply rooted in Canada, and that's not even for the Caucasian population. In the Black community, in the First Nations community. It's across the board,' he says.

For Toor, it's hockey's culture, not the sport itself, that has to change – a point emphasized during that roundtable at Queen's. Hockey as practised, he says, 'is like a very exclusive country club that doesn't let anyone in.'

The door may have cracked open just a bit. Toor has been working with the GTHL, invited to speak about inclusion and diversity. And when Don Cherry went on a racist rant about immigrants and hockey on national television in 2019 – and was fired as a result – reporters sought Toor out to speak about questions of race and diversity.

• • •

The organization where these problems are most evident is, of course, the NHL and the minor leagues that support it. They have terrible stats on diversity and inclusion. When the Institute for Diversity and Ethics in Sport released a report in 2020 measuring racial and gender diversity hiring, the NHL opted not to participate, even though the NBA, Major League Baseball, and the NFL all took part.

The NHL probably knew how poorly it would fare in terms of the number of players of colour. At one point, in the early 2010s, that number was in the single digits. Kim Davis, the NHL's executive vice-president of social impact, growth initiatives, and legislative affairs, defended the league's record in a 2019 interview. She said the NHL, at that time, had 'twenty-seven active Black players, with another eighteen coming through the system.' Above all, the NHL had a plan of action that would continue diversifying the hockey community.

In the NHL's defence, Toor says the league is working on its problems: 'I think the National Hockey League itself has the right intentions. Like, I don't disagree with that.' He's had conversations with Davis, a Black woman, about ways forward.

In an NHL policy paper called 'Shifting Demographics and Hockey's Future,' Davis and co-author William Frey wrote about how changing demographics would affect the league's future. 'The NHL recently celebrated its centennial and diversity may become the game's defining characteristic of the next 100 years,' the document states. 'The NHL is the most international of America's four major professional leagues, with the largest percentage of players from outside North America. Hockey still has a perception as 'not for some' and 'only for others,' but it is more important than ever that hockey and its leaders focus on the anticipated demographic and cultural changes.'

The policy brief argues that growing the game needs to be 'intentional,' which includes introducing the value of the game to parents who may not have played as children. I read that to mean the countless parents from marginalized communities.

The league's brain trust, and executives like Davis, may have acknowledged the dilemma. But for Toor, the real problems lie elsewhere, and likely remain unaddressed. 'The NHL and the other thirty-two teams, in my opinion, are not on the same page,' he says. 'The teams don't give a crap about diversifying the game or reaching out to different communities or expanding the game. And if the clubs don't care, their players don't give a shit either.'

II

KARL SUBBAN'S PHILOSOPHY OF LIFE, HOCKEY, AND INCLUSION

When I reflect on the state of hockey in this country and the half-hearted efforts by the hockey establishment to confront the sport's demons, I find myself thinking about the Subban family, and, specifically, how Pernell-Karl (P.K.), Malcolm, and Jordan have persevered in this game regardless of all the racial issues. I also think about how their dad, Karl, has been praised for his leadership as a teacher, coach, and ambassador of a game that has failed to embrace Black, Brown, or Indigenous players.

To widen access to hockey, we need leadership to help raise community voices. When it comes to hockey, as the sport tries to clean up its act on inclusion and discrimination, transparent and forceful leadership that pushes the envelope will be part of the solution.

Karl Subban can share a lot of insights about race and hockey; you could say he's this generation's Harry Gairey. He fell in love with the game because it helped him to both learn to love Canada and define who he was within the Canadian context. 'When I came from Jamaica, I knew Jamaica. It was my home and what I knew,' he tells me in 2020. 'I spent the first twelve years of my life there. And then here I am in this new country, where I didn't see too many people who look like me and I did not see too many people or kids playing the games that I played.'

Subban picked up baseball as a youngster because he had early dreams of being a star cricket player. But, after arriving in Canada, his introduction to hockey was an eye-opener: 'Hockey was, "Wow, wow." It was a game changer for me.'

His first years here felt strange, in a new territory. His family lived in an apartment on Peter Street in downtown Toronto. He was a curious kid. 'The Martins lived downstairs, and I remember looking outside and I didn't see one kid who looked like me,' he recalls. 'I heard some speaking and I remember turning to my parents and asking them, "What are they saying?" They said, "They're speaking French." I remember saying, "Listen, I'm never going out there." I just wanted to head back home.'

But one day, those kids asked him to play street hockey with them. 'I was a goalie because in Jamaica when I played football – that's what we called it – I was a goalie,' he says. 'I played for my school team, so I knew how to stop the ball with my feet. I was pretty coordinated. And I could catch the ball with my hand. I could even block it, pretending that I had a blocker.'

Subban immediately fell in love with the goal-tending position and idolized the Montréal Canadiens' star Ken Dryden. 'That's why I sort of – I was like a goalie, but hockey gave me friends. The most important thing in a twelve-year-old's life is usually his or her friends,' Subban tells me. 'It gave me friends right away, and especially because I was a good athlete – wow – they became my really good friends, because they all wanted me on their team. Hockey gave me something to do. Remember, in those days, we didn't have the internet and we spent a lot more time outside than we did inside.'

It also gave him a dream. At one point, he wanted to emulate his childhood sporting idol Garfield Sobers, one of the best all-rounders in cricket history. I ask Subban what it was about the game that hooked him. Hockey, he says, gave him a place to be a Canadian – but to also still be Jamaican. 'My new friends were now on my mind,' he says. 'A new sport I was playing was on my mind, and so that's where the hockey seed was planted.'

After the Subban family moved to Sudbury when he was twelve, hockey began to take up a larger role in his life – and he learned to adapt. It didn't escape him that his family was one of the very few Black families in the mining town. But that didn't bother him. 'Growing up in Sudbury is learning how to fit in and realizing that we have a lot more in common,' he said. 'You know, there are a lot more things that connect us than are working to divide us.'

Karl's father, Sylvester, and his uncle worked at the Falconbridge Mine, which was, at the time, a massive site that went down four thousand feet. Subban's parents worked hard to provide for their kids, but they couldn't afford to put their son in hockey.

He coped, and found a way to play anyway. He cheered for the Sudbury Wolves – which is a thing that bound him and Ken Dryden together – and got into rec hockey in the community. In fact, when Subban watched Wolves legend Mike Marson, the second Black Canadian in the NHL, he was sold on playing however he could manage.

But Subban also decided to pursue basketball, and he was a pretty good player for Sudbury Secondary School. He eventually found his way to Lakehead University in Thunder Bay, where he played on the men's basketball team.

'I've always felt like I've held each game in one hand,' Subban said in a 2017 interview. 'In one hand is hockey and in the other is basketball and I've always had a passion for both sports.'

At Lakehead, Subban realized his dreams of playing professional basketball weren't going to materialize. He quickly pivoted to a career in education, devoting his life to bringing out the best in his students – and, definitely, in his children.

'After graduation, I enrolled in teachers' college at Lakehead and followed my new passion,' writes Subban in his memoir, How We Did It. 'I was determined to become the best teacher I could, which led me to Toronto and a thirty-year career as a teacher and administrator, often in Toronto's toughest neighbourhoods. Those schools were where I felt I belonged, where I thought I could make the biggest impact, where I could be a difference maker.'

In Sudbury, hockey had become the glue that bound his family. But it was in Toronto where he saw how his children could excel at hockey and take it far. It fell to his oldest kids, Natasha and Nastassia, to teach young P.K. to skate. 'The thing that we did as a family was skating,' Subban says. 'My wife, Maria, skated, I skated, the girls skated.'

Their daughters, not coincidentally, became teachers. P.K. went to the NHL. 'Obviously, you have it in the back of your mind that you'd love to see them one day play in the NHL,' Subban says. 'I wish I would have had the opportunity. To play for the Sudbury Wolves – that was my NHL – but obviously that wasn't gonna happen. You're never thinking it was gonna be a possibility.'

But in Toronto, Subban was in awe of P.K.'s fortitude, and Malcolm's and Jordan's, for that matter. They wanted to push themselves as far as they could in hockey. 'They're students in the classroom, but they're also students on the ice,' he says. 'With all the people who have coached them, instructed them, worked with them, they learned what they needed to do. P.K. learned that early. He knew what he had to do.'

With a belly laugh, Subban adds, 'He learned that you can never do enough. You can never practise enough, right? You can never skate enough, you can never shoot enough pucks. He's still doing those things, because he learned what he needed to do to fulfill his dreams and fulfill his potential.'

All three of his sons played for the Belleville Bulls, a franchise located east of Toronto. Subban didn't believe it would happen until, early on, after P.K. was drafted by Belleville, he had a conversation with George Burnett, the head coach and general manager.

'He asked him, "Where did you learn to skate like that?" Then he said to us, "You're gonna play at least at the American League level." That's all I wanted to hear,' says Subban.

In a four-year career with Belleville, P.K. notched seventy-six points in fifty-six games – not bad for a defenceman known to be very physical. He was drafted by the Montréal Canadiens, Subban's childhood team – heck, P.K.'s childhood team – in the second round of the 2007 NHL draft.

Despite those successes, Subban's story, his family's story, is also about navigating race and racism within hockey. *The Color of Hockey* blog, helmed by the thoughtful and enterprising American journalist William Douglas, described the Subbans' experience with hockey racism, which goes back to when P.K. was just eight.

Douglas, quoting Karl, recounts the family's first stark experience: 'P.K. came out of the dressing room crying. He said a boy on the ice called him the N-word. We said there was no need to cry because it was only a word. We probably said something about "sticks and stones." There weren't too many kids playing who looked like P.K., but now someone had communicated it to him in a way he didn't like.'

It was a pattern that followed P.K. to the pros. During the 2014 Stanley Cup playoffs, some Boston Bruins fans reportedly sent hateful emails to P.K. and made racist social media posts after he scored two goals, including a double-overtime winner. Racism follows P.K. to this day, but his father's advice remains the same: You can't just use sticks and stones to battle against racism and discrimination. It requires leadership and intentional action.

In a CBC radio interview in late 2019, Subban recalled an incident when P.K. was still in the junior ranks and something was said to him that was overheard by the parent of another player. Karl Subban never heard it himself – in fact, he still hasn't.

'To this day, I ask him every time I see him, and he will not share it – what was said. But the important thing is that he did something,' Subban says, noting that P.K. addressed the player on his own. But these experiences hardened P.K.'s resolve to be successful – and Karl Subban's efforts to ensure the hockey world was inclusive.

'When we hear something, we need to do something or tell someone,' he told CBC Radio. 'And we need to work at erasing that fear, because that fear is a powerful, powerful thing.'

When Subban found out that Bill Peters, a coach, spewed racial epithets in the presence of Akim Aliu, a Black player, in a minor league locker room in the 2009–10 hockey season (but it was only revealed to the world ten years later), his heart and mind immediately went to Akim's safety and, by extension, the safety of all kids in the care of coaches and teachers. 'Whether they're in the classroom or in the dressing room, we want our children to be safe … It's not only about their physical safety, but also that they're mentally safe,' says Subban. Peters was subsequently fired from his job as the coach of the Calgary Flames and went on to coach in Russia.

What Aliu recounted stays with me. '[Peters] walked in before a morning pre-game skate and said, "Hey, Akim, I'm sick of you playing that n— s—,"' he said in an interview with TSN reporter Frank Seravalli, the reference being to Aliu's selection of hip-hop music. 'He said, "I'm sick of hearing this n— fucking other n— in the ass stuff." He then walked out like nothing ever happened. You could hear a pin drop in the room, everything went dead silent. I just sat down in my stall, didn't say a word.'

Aliu's account goes further. In a personal essay published on the *Players' Tribune*, he talked about how the incident triggered memories of the past, from being rammed in the mouth with a hockey stick after refusing to be hazed to the racist taunts he would hear during Quebec junior hockey games.

As a minor league coach who could make or break careers, Peters felt invincible. Said Aliu, 'Jake Dowell, our team captain, confronted him after what he did to me, but there was only so much he could do. I respect Jake for even taking my side and making a stand. But he knew that to have any future in the sport – to make money and support his family – he could only push Peters so far.'

He went on, 'Over the next few weeks I acted cold toward Peters. That was enough for him to send me away. He wrote a letter to the GM and got me sent down to the ECHL [a minor league team in the U.S.]. I was on pace to be one of the top young scorers on the team, but that didn't matter anymore. That was the full power of the oppressive hockey machine at work, in my opinion. There are hundreds of coaches at all levels of hockey in Canada and the United States just like him. They operate under the pretense of absolute power.'

Aliu, for his part, is not just devoted to persevering in his hockey career despite the racist landscape he endured. In 2020, a group of NHL players – co-chaired by Aliu and NHLer Evander Kane – formed the Hockey Diversity Alliance. Their purpose is 'to eradicate systemic racism and intolerance in hockey,' reads their mission statement online.

The HDA has made many commitments – including centring inclusivity in policy and rule changes, establishing targets for hiring and promoting Black individuals, and executing educational programming to increase awareness of racism in hockey.

The HDA's spirit of mentorship, community, and active organizing made me think of Karl Subban. He came from a different lived experience as a hockey lifer and dealt with racism in his own way. But, as a man who served for decades as a teacher and as a principal in Rexdale, responsible for schools full of students of colour and newcomer children, he understood their experiences of racism and discrimination.

I asked him how his upbringing in Canada, and his unique relationship with hockey, influenced his work as an educator. 'Because my boys are in a non-traditional sport, and they have excelled,' he says, 'I don't have a problem saying to students, "Listen, you can do whatever you want – just make up your mind to do the work. And don't let anything or anyone stop you." The other part of it is that hockey has given me the stage, and it has helped people to know me, and to see me, and to hear from me. That has worked for me wonderfully in school, when it comes to working with parents or staff or students. When I go into a new school, I'm already in the door – they know my story, I'm not a stranger, and people tend to listen. I joke on a regular basis that I'm changing my name to "P.K.'s Dad" because that's how people know me.'

There was something here that I wanted to hold on to. We trust our leaders for insight, mentorship, and experience. All of these things inform how we make decisions about future programming, education curriculums, and, yes, how we shape the field of play. For Subban, his travels, his classrooms, and his passion have given him a real chance to talk honestly with hockey people, from youth educators to executives who make decisions. 'It has opened the door for us to have conversations because people see me as someone who knows what he's doing. And so they don't hesitate to ask questions, or ask me for an opinion,' he says.

He's sought to instill an atmosphere of inclusivity in every space he's occupied. People see leaders as knowledge stewards who are essential to a fulfilling experience, in hockey and beyond. That's Karl Subban.

His point was that there's a lot of listening that needs to happen with marginalized voices — women, the disabled, and those with different religious affiliations and sexual orientations. If we can't understand how they've endured discrimination in their own lives, let alone in the hockey world, we can't prescribe ways to change those habits.

'Kids today, they have tremendous opportunities to fulfill their potential, and they have things I didn't have in terms of access to information,' Subban says. 'So God opened the door and we just want them to take advantage of it.'

12
'CRICKET PLAYS HERE'

Cricket had a massive moment in the seventies, eighties, and nineties, in urban Canada. Diasporic communities in Hamilton, Montreal, and Toronto dominated competitions, and one group, the Maverick Cricket and Social Club, stood out. The MCSC was a loose federation of clubs made up of first-generation immigrant players. Many, if not most, were Caribbean, from island nations like Trinidad and Tobago and Barbados.

Janelle Joseph, a professor at U of T's Faculty of Kinesiology and Physical Education who researches race, multiculturalism, and Indigeneity in sport, has found much to learn in understanding the GTA's expansive cricket culture and the game's intimate relationship to immigration and settlement. In 2017, she published *Sport in the Black Atlantic: Cricket, Canada and the Caribbean Diaspora*, a probing look at the role cricket played, and arguably still plays, in forging community and identity.

Her work is at least partly an attempt to capture the voices of those who were part of the great wave of West Indies migration to Greater Toronto, beginning in the 1960s.

'I went to trials for the Trinidad and Tobago team and I didn't make it,' recalled Mason, a Barbadian Canadian Joseph interviewed. 'So I say, "Let me jus' come to Canada an' start my life." I could have stayed back one year an' everyone telling me, "Stay, you'll be selected when you're older." But I just decide I want to start makin' money … At that time there were so many jobs here. They were beggin' us to come. It's just what you did. Finish A Levels [secondary school exams] and go to Canada or New York or England to find work. I get a job and make friends, that's when

I found a cricket team to play wit', so it seem everything work out. When I came to Canada first, I eventually hooked up with the West Indian community people and they encourage me to, you know, come out and have fun with them. So being new to the country I t'ink that was ... one of the focal points of me getting out and start playing cricket.'

'I didn't know that there was cricket played in Canada,' added Reggie, a Guyanese Canadian. 'I always ask and nobody ever knew ... I lived in a predominantly white neighbourhood. That was Ajax and at the time when I came there was no West Indian store. To get a West Indian store, you had to come all the way back into Scarborough ... You see a Black person in Ajax it was like, "Oh my god!" I remember one day my wife was driving down Baseline [Road] and she saw a big sign, "Cricket plays here" and "Practice on Wednesdays" ... So I went and I was the only Guyanese. All Bajans [people from Barbados] and Trinidadians, but it was comfortable, you know?'

But the cricket identity, Joseph says, remains mostly invisible in Canada's sports culture. 'The fact that many cricket players in Canada have dark skin and incorporate cultures and languages other than English as they play has resulted in their experiences being obfuscated from Canadian sport history,' she notes in her book. 'When the Mavericks left their nations of origin, most believed it would be temporary. Most played at a high level, but gave up hopes of playing professional cricket, finding competitive recreational leagues instead. Through the leagues they found a sporting outlet as well as the social capital necessary for employment, many in government-sponsored fields such as education, policing and postal services. Many developed middle-class status, friendships, and a permanent life in Canada.'

• • •

Cricket is a complicated sport. As a kid, I had a hard time with the rules and even more difficulty trying to understand the syntax of the sport. From my dad, I would hear about Garfield Sobers, a skilled 'batsman' and 'bowler' who is considered one of the sport's greatest all-around players, and Chris Gayle, one of the best batsmen in 'Twenty20' cricket but who was great in all three formats – test, Twenty20, and one-day matches. What, I wondered, was the difference between those three?

Learning to love cricket came later in life. I had to unlearn some preconceptions and work hard not to compare the game with baseball. But I've come to love watching the game and recommend others do the same. (Baseball is actually a derivative of cricket, overshadowing the game when it exerted an almost magnetic appeal on Americans during the Reconstruction.)

Here's a very condensed version of the rules: The field consists of a pitch – a twenty metre by three metre gravel rectangle – surrounded by a large oval of grass that includes both the infield and the outfield and is surrounded by the boundary. These are large spaces: regulation cricket fields can be more than twice the size, in area, of a soccer field.

Like soccer, cricket teams have eleven players a side, plus a 'twelfth man' who is sent on when a player is injured. In formal matches there are three umpires, but pickup games are just like three-on-three basketball – no refs, lots of self-policing, and a tacit agreement to play fairly.

There are three forms of the game. 'Test' matches are two innings long. Unlike baseball innings, which have three outs per side, test innings require teams to get the entire team out twice! They can last up to five days. In one-day cricket, the teams play to a fixed number of outs (usually about fifty). And in Twenty20 cricket, there are twenty outs, and games last about three hours. An out, or an over, occurs when a bowler successfully bowls six straight legal deliveries (for example, if the bowler hits the wickets or if a fielder catches a hit ball in the air).

A coin toss always determines who bats and who bowls. The aim of the batting team is to score runs while the fielding team will look to bowl ten people out to end the inning. As in baseball, fielders have area assignments if the ball comes their way: wicket-keepers, covers, gullies, and slips, etc.

Batting is done in pairs. For batters, a single run scores when a batter, after hitting the ball, is able to run from one wicket to the other. Batters can also score four or six runs by hitting or exceeding boundaries. This is as close as the sport comes to a home run, and the similarities don't end there. If you've never seen Sobers or Gayle hit sixes before, you'd be stunned by the power, pace, and trajectory of those hits. When a batter reaches one hundred runs in the pro circuits, they have hit a century.

Quite apart from its complexity, cricket is often not seen as 'Canadian' in the way hockey or football is, even though, as a colonial export, it's been played here since the eighteenth century. Given the size of the Caribbean diaspora in the GTA, that sense of otherness is strange. After all, this contingent of newcomers has had a huge impact on Canadian life and Canadian sporting life, both past and present.

For much of the first half of the twentieth century and part of the second, Canadian immigration policy was designed to keep out people of colour. The 1910 Immigration Act included the so-called 'Continuous Journey' regulation, which allowed the federal government to exclude people explicitly on the basis of race. While some restrictions were eased after World War I, the law remained restrictive, with some exceptions, including some family reunification. When it came to non-white immigrants, the borders opened a crack after World War II. Between 1955 and 1961, the West Indian Domestic Scheme enabled the first substantial influx of Caribbean immigration, mostly from Jamaica and Barbados.

The West Indian Domestic Scheme was Canada's first notable immigration policy toward the region. It limited entrance to Canada to low-wage female workers. The scheme, a key issue in 1960s Black Canadian activism, allowed mainly Jamaican and Barbadian women to come to Canada as domestic workers, nurses, and students. After one year of service, they were granted landed immigrant status, the opportunity for education and employment in other fields, and the opportunity to eventually bring other family members to Canada.

Yet Toronto activists, like Dudley Laws, Austin Clarke, Charles Roach, Winifred Gaskin, and Barbara Jones, argued that the scheme was too gendered and too restrictive, and prevented many Caribbean workers from securing permanent residency and citizenship in Canada. Even with the policy in place, immigrants faced their fair share of abuse, discrimination, and mistreatment. As the African American Intellectual History Society (AAIHS) has observed, 'the social stigma attached to domestic work had negative effects on the women who participated in the scheme. West Indian domestic workers in Toronto not only faced exclusion from white Canadian society; the low status associated with domestic work meant they also had to contend with isolation from other West Indians, living as "outsiders" among the "outsiders."'

Novelist Austin Clarke wrote about the scheme in both his fiction and non-fiction work. 'Clarke,' according to the AAIHS, 'attacked the plan for forcing West Indian women to submit to the "undignified classification of domestics" regardless of their skills and for putting massive barriers in the way of West Indian men like him who had been admitted to Canada temporarily as students and had to marry Canadian women to gain landed immigrant status instead of being admitted on their own merits.'

With immigration liberalization in the 1960s – the policy pivoted its focus from race and nationality to education and skills – about 64,000 people arrived from the Caribbean. Toronto, still largely white, experienced a rapid demographic facelift. Today, according to Statistics Canada, Canadians of Caribbean origin make up one of the largest non-European ethnic groupings in the country. They have been coming to Canada (and very much to the Greater Toronto Area) in large numbers; between 1996 and 2001, for example, the number of people of Caribbean origin rose by 11 per cent.

The sport sits at the very heart of this immigrant narrative, Joseph explains. 'Cricket was so central to their identities, to their feelings, because they lived through the 1980s and early 1990s ascendancy of the West Indies, or "Windies," as they affectionately call it. They were coming into their own as Black Canadians.'

She continues: 'People from their small islands, relatively speaking, were dominating the world in this international sport, and they had so much pride. They grew up with many of those same players. They were watching their friends – some people from their small villages – on the world stage. The fact that they felt so dominant, so in the prime of their lives … was really important – and cricket was part of that story.'

Yet Caribbean cricket was about much more than just cricket and immigration. 'The actual bat-and-ball game was important, and they would record every run and get excited about every single play,' says Joseph.

The sport provided an opportunity for Caribbean men to mark their home culture, their religious principles, their middle- and upper-class aspirations, and their views of other groups (including Indo-Caribbean and South Asian peoples and women). Many of the Mavericks were trying to establish or grow careers in education, policing, and the postal services. They didn't dwell on the historical legacy of slavery or racism, but rather affirmed their shared Black identities. With calypso music frequently on offer, Joseph tells me, tournaments and games provided a space to both socialize and network – they were 'liming,' she says. 'I sometimes thought, "If there was no cricket- ing here, these guys would still be here, talking shit on the road, eating their curry goat and patties." Cricket was almost always happening in the background.

'I saw a lot of people kind of wheeling and dealing and, you know, bringing their work to the cricket grounds, working as mortgage brokers or plumbers or, you know, whatever kind of industry they were in,' Joseph says. 'They were finding clients and keeping those networks strong to keep minding the Black commu- nity. And so there's kind of a two-sided aspect to what cricket meant for them.'

• • •

These days, cricket has spread beyond the Caribbean diaspora. According to U of T's Peter Donnelly, the sport 'now gets very connected with two big communities: South Asian and Caribbean.' But, he adds, 'it's popular with all of those South Africans and Brits and Australians and New Zealanders that are in town.' Data generated by Donnelly's GTActivity project, which tracks sports and recreation across the region, revealed that the game is being played even more broadly than he expected. 'I live in Burlington and the park has just been mowed and they pegged out a cricket field in the last three or four years,' he says when we speak in 2019.

He tells me about watching a game on Sunday afternoon in 2017. It was clearly a mixed-race team, with several South Asian players. One participant told Donnelly that the team was part of a ten- to twelve-squad league. He then spoke to a batter from St. Catharines, Ontario. 'I said, "Well, what kind of people are playing?" This is a Brown guy with a Canadian accent. He said to me, "We have people from everywhere – South Asia, West Indies, Australia, New Zealand, and Britain. You know, pretty much everybody except Canadians."' Donnelly and the batter shared a good laugh over that one. 'All these guys were Canadian!'

Such examples provide important insights into the work of building the city we want. In fact, I'd say that cricket is a piece of the puzzle we can't ignore. This sport can help us understand the newcomer experience in Canada, and it can explain how we think about forming sports cultures for communities with different experiences from those of second- and third-generation settlers.

The evolving traditions of cricket also reveal how new ideas that percolate to the surface in a profoundly diverse region in turn alter a diasporic sport. Early on, the games were mostly played by men. Women came to the cricket grounds as supporters – wives, daughters, extended family, and even mistresses provided logistical support to the matches. 'A rare few come to every game and may cook meals for the after-parties, score keep, or enjoy the Black/Caribbean cricket culture alongside male supporters,' wrote Joseph in her book. 'Other women are linked to the club only through their absence from games, attendance at dances and other social activities, or through their chauffeur and laundry services.'

These practices reflected traditional gender dynamics. Cricket pitches were places for Afro-Caribbean masculinities to be on full display, including some denigrating banter and homophobia. Women didn't play the sport. 'What [do] they do on summer weekends when they are not at games and with whom?' Joseph wrote. 'What are their experiences at club dances and fundraisers? What are the roles and experiences of white or East-Asian-Canadian women who marry into the Afro-Caribbean culture celebrated by the Mavericks? What types of opportunities are available for women who would prefer to be players rather than supporters?'

Today, their daughters may be the ones batting and bowling. In Scarborough, on campuses at U of T Scarborough, Centennial College, Seneca, and Durham College, women's cricket has carved out a place in the sports landscape.

In March 2018, U of T Scarborough hosted its first ever tri-series women's cricket tournament at the Toronto Pan Am Sports Centre. The school welcomed two other cricket clubs from Wilfrid Laurier University and Ryerson University. In a report on the series, Shireen Ahmed, a sports journalist I deeply respect, noted the camaraderie between women players, many of colour, as well as the massive support they received from the wider cricket community in Canada.

Cricket is creating an important space for women of colour in university sport, Ahmed wrote in *University Affairs*. To maintain that space, players need to advocate for more options on campuses, either through varsity teams or student clubs. 'I believe that for cricket – and specifically for women's cricket – to grow, [we need] to minimize the idea that we need hyper-masculine, monopolizing sport empires and instead empower every sport to their maximum potential,' UTSC captain Perenthaa Arulnesan told Ahmed.

So far, however, few universities have official student cricket clubs such as those at Ryerson, UTSC, and Laurier. 'The players say that for their cricket programs to thrive,' Ahmed wrote, 'it's imperative that their teams, and the sport more generally, be formally recognized by Ontario University Athletics, the governing body for interuniversity sport in the province.'

The arrival of women's cricket isn't the only way in which the sport is changing. Black diaspora communities are not playing cricket like the first generation. A lot of student athletes, weekend rec-leaguers, and casual athletes in these communities have taken up basketball, or hockey, or baseball.

Meanwhile, as an older generation of Caribbean-Canadian cricket players retires, athletes representing a younger generation from another diaspora, South Asia, have arrived on GTA cricket pitches. In recent years, Joseph observes, 'there are more and more South Asian players on their fields and in their practice spaces. So it's also this kind of conversation as you think about multiculturalism, multiple diasporas, and interactions among guests coming in from different places.' The conversation is not necessarily about who plays what, but rather more essential questions about how and where.

Dedicated space for cricket, after all, has always been scarce, and thus serves as a limiting factor in the sport's popularity. Within the City of Toronto, there is one brick-and-mortar club to be reckoned with: the Toronto Cricket Skating and Curling Club, which is as old as the University of Toronto. (The elite private club also programs tennis, lawn bowling, and other British colonial sports.)

According to the Toronto District Cricket Association, only a handful of decent fields can be found in the inner suburbs. The Eglinton Flats, for example, is a go-to facility for a lot of communities; many Caribbean players regard 'Egg Flats' as the mecca of cricket in Toronto. But the list of suitable spaces is short. If you find kids and teens playing cricket in the city, they're probably using narrow, cramped, or even paved spaces. Demand, on the other hand, is soaring. A lot of Torontonians want a place to play cricket. About 90,000 were on recreation program waitlists in 2006, and that number grew to about 200,000 in 2016. The city predicts that demand will double again by 2026.

In a city-region with a surplus of underused ice rinks and softball diamonds, the burgeoning ranks of cricket fans – all those young players who inherited a diasporic sport popularized two generations ago by the Mavericks and their followers – have to make do with spaces that are at best adequate. That's what we do. But is it enough?

13

THE CURIOUS INTERSECTION OF POLITICS AND CRICKET

It has become one of the most ironic and iconic political snapshots in recent Toronto history. On a sunny day, Doug Ford and John Tory – now premier and mayor – stand on a field, mugging for a camera. Which isn't especially unusual, except in this case, the joke involves the mayor bending over slightly while the premier administers a bit of a spanking. They're both in their cricket whites, and Tory's got shin pads on. The tool of choice is a cricket bat.

The image, all in good fun, turned out to be the perfect visual metaphor for critics of the soon-to-be mayor, who felt he was always coming in for some political discipline from the big boys at Queen's Park.

That encounter between Ford and Tory wasn't a coincidence, much less a one-off. For many years, mayoral politics and cricket in Toronto have intersected in fascinating ways. The mayor of Toronto has traditionally been actively involved in the annual CIMA Mayor's Trophy, which is part of a community initiative created by the Chartered Institute of Management Accountants, an international professional association. CIMA's community initiatives revolve around cricket: a school tournament and cricket-oriented scholarships for youth from diverse neighbourhoods. The Mayor's Trophy event, one of the largest in Canada, has grown in popularity over the years and is lauded by the sport's global organizing body, the International Cricket Council (ICC).

Typically held at Sunnybrook Park, the tournament is well attended: the chief of police, lots of corporate CEOs, and media personalities turn out, as well as plenty of schools and local teams. Adam Vaughan, a well-known broadcaster turned politician, has played for years, and counts himself as a vocal supporter of the cup. The event traces back to the tenure of Mayor David Miller, who is a sports buff. 'He was the person who put the Mayor's Cup together,' Vaughan recalls. 'He understood it instinctively. He gave it the support, worked with CIMA to raise the profile, and put the Mayor's Cup in play to get the schoolboys playing as well, and then the schoolgirls.' Miller, Vaughan adds for the record, is a damn good cricket player. 'Dave is a much better batsman, much better athlete than I am. He's much stronger.'

Tellingly, the Ford brothers were also hearty participants in the cup – it was a rare point of agreement with Miller. Though Rob and Doug were famously into football, they fully understood the effect that team sports like cricket can have on young athletes.

Vaughan's connection to the game runs deep and travels to intriguing places. It began with his dad, Colin Vaughan, an architect turned politician turned broadcaster. Born in Australia, Colin arrived in Toronto in the mid-fifties. He wasn't a big cricket player. 'He was more of a swimmer,' Vaughan says. 'But my mom was a huge tennis player and the only place to play tennis was at the Toronto Cricket Club.'

As soon as the members of the club heard his dad's accent, they put him in to bat, Vaughan recalls with a laugh. 'My earliest childhood memories are watching my dad play cricket. I used to have his sweater. I used to have his cap for a while, too. The cricket gloves he used for hockey gloves, for street hockey, were great.'

It was through the cricket club that Colin made connections that had lasting effects on the city, including one with a provincial cabinet minister named Roy McMurtry, who helped pull the levers that halted the Spadina Expressway. Colin made another important link through cricket – to the novelist and essayist Austin Clarke. They met post-match at an old haunt on College Street called Whiffle Club. Says Vaughan: 'They were lifelong friends from there and after – debating two things: who was a better

French cook and whether the Australians were better than the West Indians [in cricket].'

Vaughan rekindled his love for the game in his forties as a member of a media team. He realized that a lot of participants played at a high level, but within clubs formed by corporations, such as major accounting firms or other institutions, like the Toronto Police Service. 'There are all these other professional organizations that also play cricket into the cross-currents of the club system,' he explains. 'It's a way of sustaining the old school networks, which are really strong – in terms of what school you went to, in Trinidad, or Jamaica, or Barbados, or the professional class and the university area, as well.'

· · ·

David Miller's almost fanatical interest in soccer is well-known. While in office, he led a push to build BMO Field, the home of Toronto Football Club. But Miller also asked Vaughan to develop a cricket strategy for the city. Miller had made a pledge to build a certain number of cricket pitches across the city. Besides the CIMA tournament, he'd seen the huge turnouts for the festival-like cricket matches at Eglinton Flats and the Maple Leaf Cricket Club, which is in King City, a town just north of the GTA. 'They weren't just a sporting event,' Miller tells me. 'It was a community event.'

The importance of the sport among diaspora communities, for Miller, represented a crucial city-building challenge: the city, he felt, had to think creatively and deeply about how to accommodate a space-intensive sport like cricket within a crowded urban area. 'How do we find ways to use this space for multiple users?' he asked. 'Can you have the cricket pitches and soccer pitches in the same place and keep the wicket protected?'

Vaughan had the same question, and the answer led him to make a daring and unexpected proposal in 2013: put a cricket pitch in Coronation Park, located across from the Princes' Gates, south of Lake Shore Boulevard. The park had long been one of

Toronto's primary sports fields. It contains three softball diamonds and an off-leash dog area. With a properly placed wicket pitch, the park was also the perfect size for cricket.

To get it done, the city would have had to rejig the existing baseball diamonds to accommodate a cricket pitch. Vaughan, the local councillor, said the idea wouldn't lead to the loss of a baseball diamond and wouldn't cost that much. He also wanted to fit out the venue so the pitch could be turned into a stadium when needed for major events, such as Caribana, the annual Caribbean carnival festival that culminates in a joyous, vibrant Grande Parade on the first weekend of August, just in time for Emancipation Day. (The festival, which averages over 1.2 million attendees every year, is the largest of its kind in Canada. Its economic benefits are more than impressive – in 2014, Caribana produced an economic windfall for the city worth $338 million.)

The plan surfaced just as Canada's national cricket team was hitting its stride internationally and looking to qualify for tournaments. 'The cricketers wanted a bigger pitch,' recalls Vaughan, 'and they were looking for a downtown one with change rooms.'

The story loops back to all those corporate and institutional teams in the city, and the way the teams forge connections with one another and political figures. Local business leaders at the time were looking to bring high-performance cricket exhibitions to Toronto, featuring well-known international stars playing with homegrown players.

Roy Singh, who runs a Bay Street gold exploration company, lobbied Vaughan and the city to bid for a tournament that could be held at the Rogers Centre, featuring a somewhat shorter and more exciting form of cricket known as Twenty20 or T20. 'The T20 format is exciting. It's sexy. It keeps you on the edge of your seat,' Singh says. 'People love the Maple Leafs. Fans love excitement. I think this format will adapt very well here.'

A T20 tournament in August made sense to Vaughan. In cricket-loving South Asia, August is monsoon season. 'No one's playing cricket and everyone wants to watch cricket,' says

Vaughan. He felt the tournament would represent a critical mass moment for the sport, with high-octane teams from the Caribbean and South Asia taking part and being televised back in India, Pakistan, and Sri Lanka.

The mere prospect of such an event triggered a surge of interest, Vaughan recounts. 'I had about fifty or sixty people call me, saying that they were groundskeepers back in Karachi or Bombay, or they grew up around the Queen's Park Oval [a hallowed cricket patch located in Trinidad] and their uncle was the groundskeeper.' Many even volunteered to tend the grounds – maintain the wickets, take care of the batting nets (which would keep the ball from rolling onto Lake Shore Boulevard) – if the idea went ahead.

'You can employ these old guys who want to do nothing more than just talk cricket and fiddle around with the netting,' Vaughan says. 'Part of what we were trying to do with the National Stadium was create a cabinet that was fit for an international standard pitch – an ICC pitch.'

Unfortunately, that vision, and the excitement it inspired, never came to fruition. The momentum dissipated, and city hall's focus shifted to football – the sport that was a religion to Rob Ford, Miller's successor. With the T20 tournament bid deadline approaching, city officials couldn't find a suitable venue and didn't have time to transform Coronation Park to satisfy the requirements of the International Cricket Council.

Other X factors surfaced. With Coronation Park, Vaughan recounts, 'all the trees around the outside of that park were planted one by one at the end of World War I by returning veterans of the Canadian Army. Even though they'd fallen into disrepair and we could take five or six of them down, it was seen as sacrilege.'

Vaughan tried but failed to find an alternate solution. What's more, he was leaving city council for federal politics; absent a champion in the city, the plan looked like it would die on the vine. Even cricket's highly placed friends couldn't, or wouldn't, come to the rescue. 'It was a possibility for a moment,' he says, 'and then it wasn't.'

14

GO GREEN: THE BIG CIRCLE
WHERE CRICKET, ECOLOGY,
AND GENDER MET

If you want to see the future of cricket in Toronto, check out the playing fields of Valley Park, a little school with a big presence. Located on Overlea Boulevard, Valley Park Middle School sits right beside the Don River, close to a lot of nature. Nestled between Thorncliffe Park (to the west) and Flemingdon Park (to the north), it serves the needs of about 1,200 middle school students, who together speak more than fifty languages. Planned communities built in the 1960s, these two enclaves, with more than thirty apartment towers, are some of the most multicultural neighbourhoods in Canada.

According to the city's 2016 neighbourhood profile of Flemingdon Park, for example, 64 per cent of residents are immigrants – well above the city average of 50 per cent. And the Thorncliffe Neighbourhood Office, a multi-service agency, says the area is home to newcomers from Pakistan, India, Philippines, Colombia, Sudan, and Afghanistan.

Reflecting its demographic profile, Valley Park had space set aside for cricket – although, as of the early 2010s, most of it was being used for portable classrooms. The school's interest in the sport also extended beyond its East York catchment area.

In 2011, Indian cricketer Sunil Joshi and his Pakistani counterpart, Wasim Akram – dubbed the 'Wayne Gretzkys of cricket' – came to the school to greet the kids. Brought to Canada by the Royal Bank of Canada (RBC) to engage with children and market the game, Joshi and Akram spent a week mentoring young Canadian players. 'I've always believed in youth cricket because they are the ones who are going to [play] in the future and get laurels for their country,' Joshi, a former Indian national team star, told the *Globe and Mail*. (RBC is an active supporter of cricket in Canada, funding school teams, sponsoring new fields, and donating equipment and instruction to more than 1,100 schools, including many in the GTA.)

These guys were good – still are. Joshi was an all-rounder who excelled in all the different forms of cricket and then became a coach, managing Indian teams and consulting others in Oman and Bangladesh. Akram, nicknamed the 'Sultan of Swing,' is considered one of the best bowlers in the sport's history, the first player ever to achieve five hundred wickets in one-day cricket.

During his visit, Akram offered up a remark about our national team that stuck with me: 'They look very talented, but obviously the structure is not there in Canada.' In a city-region like Greater Toronto, 'structure' is another way of talking about the social and physical ecosystem of sports – the local leagues, the rep leagues, the coaching networks, the parents, media and corporate attention, the spaces to play and practise – all are part of the puzzle. And unlike in hockey and basketball, some of those pieces were missing for cricket in Toronto. What Akram may not have known is that the Valley Park community was determined to push back against that narrative.

• • •

The story starts with Lisa Grogan-Green, a cheerful presence whose kids attended a North Toronto public school nowhere near Valley Park. In the late 1990s, she was involved with a playground restoration/landscaping project at Bedford Park Public School. Through a neighbour's involvement with the Toronto Region Conservation Authority, she met a legendary Toronto landscape architect named Michael Hough and enlisted his help.

Born in France, Hough had worked on projects like Ontario Place and Philosopher's Walk, next to the Royal Ontario Museum, and eventually founded the University of Toronto's landscape architecture program. In the late 1980s, he became a consultant for former Toronto mayor David Crombie's Royal Commission on the Future of the Toronto Waterfront. Crombie later appointed him chair of the Environment Work Group studying the future of the Lower Don Lands, and Hough eventually wrote a book about the Don River.

In 2009, Grogan-Green invited Hough and Valley Park principal Nick Stefanoff out for lunch. Stefanoff had been the principal at Bedford Park when the playground was being restored, and they'd stayed in touch. The conversation turned to schoolyard landscaping. Stefanoff said some of the teachers at Valley Park wanted to build a tulip garden, Grogen-Green remembers. But he wanted to try something more ambitious, more environmentally conscious, like what he and Grogan-Green had done at Bedford. Hough suggested that whatever was proposed should connect the school to the Don. 'So we came up with this idea of rooftop rainwater harvesting – we wanted to take all the rainwater and divert it, and use it to irrigate the cricket field,' she says.

That plan turned out to be too ambitious, but it nonetheless amplified the growing interest at the school, among both students and teachers, in expanding Valley Park's cricket programming. 'The vice-principal at the school was a cricket coach,' Grogan-Green says, 'and they were joking about how popular cricket was – and if there was an away game, they'd have a hundred parent drivers.'

What happened next was a confluence of goodwill, good funding, and good timing. According to U of T's School of Cities, planning for renovations began in earnest in 2010. 'To date, more than $2.5 million in capital has been privately fundraised through a community-led effort to build this outdoor facility,' says their website. In the process, the school's appetite for cricket got the attention of mayoral candidates during the 2014 municipal election. 'A lot of the cricket organizations were using that race as an

Dating back to Toronto's early days as a British colony, cricket has been played by generations of Torontonians, from fancy clubs to wide, broad schoolyards and fields. (Courtesy of Go Green Youth Centre)

opportunity to advocate for cricket and having more playing fields and having them maintained better,' Grogan-Green recalls. What's more, the appetite among cricket fans for a venue suitable for hosting an international event hadn't abated.

Local and provincial politicians, among them then-premier and Don Valley West MPP Kathleen Wynne, helped the school raise $750,000 from the city, the Trillium Foundation, and other donors to begin the process of transforming the sports fields behind Valley Park into a proper cricket pitch – a process that produced a striking transformation of what was once a standard-issue schoolyard and part of a nearby hydro corridor. The space would include a regulation-size high-performance natural turf cricket field, a clay running track, a multi-sport court, amphitheatre seating, a baseball diamond, a bioswale, a constructed wetland with a viewing deck, and meadow and forest areas.

In 2017, the field was renamed the Go Green Youth Centre – and is now run by a full-fledged youth-focused charity. The centre's mission is to support disadvantaged youth, especially children of recent immigrants, assisting them in overcoming social exclusion and isolation. Go Green operates free multi-sport and enriched recreational programs for children from Flemingdon Park and Thorncliffe Park, and is permitted to use the space –

with the school board's blessing – on weekdays after school and on Saturdays.

Its board is headed by people in the community. Grogan-Green was the co-chair as of 2021. The centre is run by teens who live in and grew up in the area, and interest in cricket is as clear as can be. 'We [in 2017] had just expanded our camps pretty dramatically from the five cricket players to 150 kids – and now we have 300,' she tells me in a 2020 interview.

• • •

Just before the pandemic, Go Green took an important step: it started programming cricket for girls. The organization has also sought to introduce its young participants to professional women cricket players. In 2018, they brought Sana Mir, one of the world's best cricket bowlers, to visit at nearby Thorncliffe Park Public School. Throngs of children attended the meet-up, with Mir providing a workshop to forty girls afterward.

In 2017, Shahid Afridi, former captain of the Pakistan National team, helped turn on the LED sports lights for the first time at Go Green with former Ontario Premier Kathleen Wynne. (Courtesy of Go Green Youth Centre)

'It was one of the best receptions in any school I've got … I love the enthusiasm of the kids,' Mir, who regularly ranks near the top of the International Cricket Council women's one-day international bowling rankings, told a local news site. 'I'm a big, big advocate of sports. It's a wonderful way of teaching kids leadership, teamwork, and discipline … all in a very fun environment.'

In a male-dominated sport, and in a community where gender roles are still very traditional, the advent of girls' cricket is no small accomplishment, and one that didn't happen on its own.

In 2019, the youth centre caught Lauren Wolman's attention. She had just finished her doctoral research, founded a sports development consultancy, and was working as a social innovation research manager for Centennial College. Wolman also loves rugby.

Her research focus has long been on inclusive sport practices and sport participation among young people, especially those living in communities with higher rates of unemployment, lower income, newcomers, and visible minorities. 'I believe that sport is a medium to have various social outcomes,' she tells me. 'However, we know that kids don't have access or feel included within sport. Some of it is literal – physically, as in *I can't afford it,* or *It's too far.* And then there's socially: even if it was available to them, even if it was cheaper, even if it was close, they're still not going.'

And finally there's gender: 'We always have to be mindful of gender because what happens for boys doesn't happen for girls.' If you intersect gender with other identities, like being Muslim, Grogan-Green says, it's even less likely they will feel included.

Go Green and Valley Park were on Wolman's radar because she couldn't ignore them. She coached girls' rugby at Marc Garneau Collegiate, which is across the street. In her first year,

The advent of women and girls' cricket is across the GTA has been profound, with people of all ages taking part on post-secondary campuses, among other locales. (Courtesy of Go Green Youth Centre)

she attracted a lot of girls to the team, and some went on to play in the rugby club system. But then, the next year, all the girls dropped out. The reasons: hijabs, Ramadan, boys. It was, she says, a 'very dynamic' situation, and upsetting.

She wondered whether the girls were valuing the sport at all. Unlike many boys, she says, the girls 'were not embedded [in sports]. They're not culturally conditioned to think, "I'm gonna play sport and do well at school."'

From her research and work in Thorncliffe and Flemingdon, Wolman also knew that even when sport opportunities were in place, both inside and outside of school, participation rates varied significantly. 'Thorncliffe has a lot of sports bases, they have an arena, they have a baseball diamond, and now a cricket field. They have soccer fields and all these

The Go Green cricket field.
(Courtesy of Go Green Youth Centre)

things, right? But if you ask who are the kids using them at prime hours, it's white kids,' she says. The reason? Youth sports clubs from elsewhere in the city have been securing permits to use the facilities for years. 'The only time the local kids can use it is actually when it's not permitted: nighttime. Well, there's a problem with nighttime, particularly in Flemingdon and particularly for girls.' Despite the new cricket pitch, a lot of kids still play cricket in parking lots, courtyards, and in between buildings, she says.

Wolman's dissertation focuses on the 'sports journeys' of local kids – the challenges of being from an immigrant family and intersecting with sports, how space influences sports participation, and all the gender challenges. She shared her findings with local kids, their parents, and the Go Green staff. Ultimately, Wolman says, the effectiveness of Go Green's cricket program should rival those of the Hijabi Ballers, the Toronto Inner-City

Rugby Foundation, and the Impact Skateboard club – all groups that put a high premium on inclusiveness that involves girls.

While cricket has muscled its way into the sports landscape of dense and diverse communities like Thorncliffe and Flemingdon Park, Wolman says there are still hurdles to overcome. While there's a full week of multi-sport programming available for boys, only one time slot is available for girls between the ages of twelve and eighteen (as of 2021). To paraphrase the old baseball cliché, build it, and some will come. 'Cricket's great,' as Wolman says, 'but for who?'

15

AJAHN SUCHART'S OLYMPIC AMBITIONS

Greater Toronto has fostered many great examples of sports movements, but one in particular goes way beyond the latest fitness craze. Its popularity across Canada has been sparked by a community in Toronto – and, arguably, one man's grit. Indeed, his passion helped propel the sport to Olympic recognition for the 2024 games.

• • •

Muay Thai gyms are a beautiful thing to see – and smell. One, in the Lansdowne and Bloor area, sits above an auto collision garage and is accessed by a narrow stairway. It has boxing rings, punching bags, and some mirrors that don't quite reach the ceilings. This place should smell like sweat but it doesn't. The students going through drills here, though dripping wet, keep the place clean, from the gloves and pads to the mats.

Mostly, this gym is all about the energy coming off the fighters, both men and women. They line up like soldiers working their way through drills. As a couple of chaps prep the ropes and strike pads, a fit, moderately sized man steps away from his students and walks over to me. He is fitted out with athletic gear and wears a wide smile. Though in his sixties, Ajahn Suchart Yodkerepauprai looks half that age. His handshake is soft and meaty, and his body language isn't intense. He's happy to chat.

'This is a standard Muay Thai gym,' he says. *Ajahn* is a Thai term meaning teacher or professor. Suchart is the founder of Siam No. 1, the oldest Muay Thai gym in Canada.

He hasn't always been at this location. He opened his first gym in Toronto in 1992, in the basement of the Young Thailand restaurant at Gerrard and Jarvis. He moved to other locations – including St. Clair West, Vaughan Road, and Bloordale – before settling in High Park in 2020.

Over decades as a Muay Thai instructor, Suchart has taught about fifty thousand students, including thousands in his Toronto-based gyms. He has helped build the careers of first responders, teachers, and professional fighters. Many of his proteges, themselves krus (the Thai word for teacher), have opened their own schools in the GTA, won professional championships, and are building larger communities for this sport. Most importantly, his students are sharing his teachings in their own gyms – teachings that now seed the future of the sport in Canada. All of this is Suchart's legacy.

'I want to use Muay Thai to build role models for my community first and hopefully become a society,' he tells me, as the sparring session gets underway.

Every kru who earned their stripes with Ajahn Suchart is an ambassador of his culture in this city and beyond – and their gyms are burgeoning hubs of community, he says. In the next few years, Muay Thai could be an Olympic sport. It has taken twenty years to grow this community in Toronto. Talking to him, I felt I had stumbled onto something incredible.

• • •

Muay Thai, a.k.a. Thai boxing, is a martial art that goes well beyond punching. Kicks, clinches, and elbow and knee strikes are also allowed. It demands a great deal of conditioning and discipline, which is the first goal of the drills at Siam No. 1.

Have you seen a match? I can't begin to describe how the sport is so many things at once, including poetic and spiritual. You see native Thais pray in their corners and wear ceremonial gear on their arms and heads. A few moments later, those same fighters will snap roundhouse kicks that can break bones or land elbow-punch combos that could open up nasal cavities.

If there's anything I ask of anyone getting to know a sport, it is that they understand what it represents. I say this because Muay Thai is more than just about powerful hits and pain. It's a sport that is intimately connected to the Thai people – a martial art that embodies their culture and history, which is where Suchart's story begins.

Before he came to Toronto as a young adult, Suchart grew up and fought in the mountains of Mae Hong Son, in Thailand's northwest. The mountainous terrain equated with humble beginnings for Suchart. He was raised in an impoverished village without running water. He didn't own a bicycle until he was eight years old.

The sport is an inherited practice for many Thai children. By the time he was nine, Suchart was competing in Muay Thai competitions in his village community. 'Thai boys start to learn to fight probably at about seven, eight, nine years old without a gym,' he says. 'We learn it from school, but they teach you. Not only the curriculum but the activities of Thai people and Thai boys.' Muay Thai is as essential to Thai culture as religion, he explains. In a country with temples everywhere, Muay Thai is a way of life, and generations of Thais get together to observe. 'Everybody participates – number one, in religion and belief in religion; number two, culture; and three, activity.'

I believe that. Outside of Thailand, the sport is necessary to keep Thai people – young and old – connected to their communities, families, and maybe even the land itself.

When he was seven years old, the sport found him as he was looking for answers. His mother had died when he was about three. His father had remarried and was preparing to move away, but Suchart decided to stay in his home village. 'I said, "Dad, I'm not going to follow you. I've gotta stay here,"' he recalls, with a light quiver in his voice. A remarkable moment of autonomy for a child, but he wanted to be in a place where he felt comfortable, and that place was his school and Muay Thai.

Eventually, Suchart enrolled in an all-boys Catholic boarding school in the Chiang Mai region. Because he had been given so many challenges at a young age, he knew he could take on this new environment with ease.

And boy, did he ever. He turned pro at fourteen, sparring and fighting against Chiang Mai kids his age and a little older, often in the schoolyard, bare-knuckled. In 1982 and 1983, when he was in his early twenties, Suchart became the Northern Thailand Champion and held the title for two years, an unprecedented achievement.

Before Suchart moved to Canada in 1987, he began competing internationally. Yet he had also sworn a commitment to Muay Thai that went beyond competition. He earned a bachelor's degree in physical education, graduating with honours from the Chiang Mai Physical Education and Teachers College. He taught physical education in local schools for a few years and leveraged that experience to begin teaching Muay Thai. Suchart eventually became one of only a few professional Muay Thai masters in Thailand who had also earned a formal academic degree.

When he moved to Toronto, he swore to himself that Muay Thai would continue to be part of his life. It was his life's passion, and he wanted to put this knowledge to effective use. Most of all, Suchart wanted to elevate traditional Muay Thai into the mainstream fight culture in this country.

In Suchart's view, North American fight culture has dismissed the spiritual and philosophical principles of Muay Thai. There's a lot to unpack here, but it begins with simple ideas about what Muay Thai is and what those principles mean to the identity of the sport itself.

'Muay Thai is the heritage of Thai people,' Suchart tells me. 'You know, we've participated in this culture for over two thousand years. For Canadians and Americans, they look at the business only – they don't look at heritage, they don't look at the culture.' But, he says, they see the sport as a means of education – and something that can be passed on to the next generation.

'In Ontario, I had about eighty-three affiliations [krus], and their path is 75 to 80 per cent to run the business. But they forget about where the business, the base, came from,' he says. Ambassadors of the sport – gym owners, krus, and the like – 'came from education, came from martial arts, from sport, from the corporate world. They can run a business without the foundation of culture, martial art, and sport. But it's missing there. They look at it as just their job.'

Whether it is rules or competition formation, Suchart continues to push for these principles. But he still has a lot of work to do to make sure his standards for the sport stay in place.

In Suchart's view, whenever a kru makes small adjustments to take care of the sport's traditional practices, then Muay Thai will be in a good place. Over the years, in fact, he has been an excellent judge of character and knows how to distinguish the people who come into the sport looking to honestly connect with its foundations from those who just see Muay Thai as a means to make money. 'I've been teaching for the last twenty-seven years, in over thirty-six countries. I want Canadians and Americans to understand that Muay Thai is a business but that it came from the base of culture and martial art and sport of Thailand.'

• • •

Many forms of martial arts have long faced struggles to gain legitimacy, including regulatory approval, in Ontario. For example, mixed martial arts (MMA) was only legalized in 2011, and its place in the province's sports culture was, at best, marginal. As then-premier Dalton McGuinty told the Canadian Press at the time, it 'just wasn't a priority for Ontario families.'

The concern was fighter safety. When the premier finally changed his mind, the government said it needed to regulate MMA in order to keep the fighters safe. 'We have always said that we would be monitoring mixed martial arts and we have been doing that for some time,' MPP Sophia Aggelonitis, who was consumer services minister at the time, told the Canadian Press. 'We need to have a system in place where we regulate it; that's the only way I can control the safety of competitors.'

Consequently, many Canadian pro fighters had to fight outside of Ontario to make ends meet. All the while, the heavily commercialized Ultimate Fighting Championship (UFC) was having a lot of success in Vancouver and Montreal, where main card pay-per-view broadcasts generated millions of dollars in revenue. To this day, MMA fight culture is so much more vibrant in Quebec and the Maritimes than in Ontario. I remember covering some fight cards in Nova Scotia with fighters who had more than a puncher's chance in the UFC. The attendance was robust, the fandom enthusiastic.

When Ontario looked at accommodating MMA, it had to contend with the sport's popularity, but also Section 83 of the federal Criminal Code. It's a piece of criminal law that Suchart, Muaythai Ontario, and every other member group have had to navigate, and it has to do with the fact that some 'prize fighting' is illegal.

The legal definition reads as follows:

83(2) In this section, 'prize fight' means an encounter or fight with fists or hands between two persons who have met for that purpose by previous arrangement made by or for them, but a boxing contest between amateur sportsmen, where the contestants wear boxing gloves of not less than one hundred and forty grams each in mass, or any boxing contest held with the permission or under the authority of an athletic board or commission or similar body established by or under the authority of the legislature of a province for the control of sport within the province, shall be deemed not to be a prize fight.

(While Section 83(2) is federal jurisdiction, provinces – and municipalities in Alberta, New Brunswick, and the Northwest Territories – administer sports like kickboxing and boxing. Legalizing MMA meant ensuring that Section 83 was applicable the sport – that is, subject to regulation in order to protect fighters.)

At first, legislators thought MMA was not prize fighting as per the Criminal Code definition, even though the province had already legalized kickboxing. But Ontario couldn't deny the sport's popularity or profits – and it announced, as of January 1, 2011, that applications for MMA events could be accepted. (Eventually, in 2013, sports like MMA, but also karate and tae kwon do, were legalized under Section 83. It was the first time the Criminal Code section on prize fighting had been changed since 1934.) Eventually, UFC had its first main card in spring 2011 at the Rogers Centre – an event that was considered one of the biggest in-stadium MMA draws ever. 'It's been a long time coming and we're thrilled,' Marc Ratner, the UFC vice-president of regulatory and government affairs, told the Canadian Press. 'Ontario,' he added, 'is a very, very important market to us. Canada is the mecca of the sport. Toronto is one of the MMA cities in the world.'

In my opinion, Toronto could also become a north star for Muay Thai – the urban standard bearer for the sport in North America. But what I've found is that Muay Thai athletes, just like MMA fighters, still have to travel out of country to compete.

In 2017, when Simon Marcus, one of Suchart's most successful students, was preparing for a world championship fight in the GLORY World Series, one of the top kickboxing promotions on the planet, he trained in Toronto. According to a *Toronto Star* story written by Morgan Campbell, a great sportswriter, the event offered Marcus a chance to become a crossover kickboxing star. 'My goal is to maximize my popularity within kickboxing and make the sport as popular as possible,' Marcus told Campbell at his North York gym. 'I'm going to market myself while I can, but mainly it's about living my dream, which is fighting.'

With one caveat: Marcus, who is considered a legend in his sport, has never fought a professional fight in Toronto or anywhere near the country of his upbringing. In 2010, he had to relocate to Thailand to train alongside Buakaw Banchamek, one of the sport's best-known fighters and ambassadors. 'I needed to go somewhere where I was surrounded by fighters who were serious,' he says. 'It catapulted me in terms of recognition.'

Toronto can certainly be a place for serious fighters, those who have dreams like Marcus's. Professor Peter Donnelly's GTACtivity project offered proof that Toronto could be a place for many kinds of sports practices. UFC's legalization opened the door for Muay Thai's stewards, Ajahn Suchart included. It was a chance for passionate practitioners and policy-makers to show their community what they brought to the neighbourhood.

• • •

What Suchart seeks is not an unreasonable ask. For him, the strong connection to the Thai people, and the benefits in terms of fitness and discipline, not only define the sport, but should also give it a legitimate place in Toronto's and Ontario's sporting landscape. Without these principles, the sport is basically like all the other forms of kickboxing in North America.

During our interview, Suchart drew the distinction between Muay Thai and those other sports. 'In my country, particularly at professional levels, 97 per cent of matches go five rounds, because there's so much skill – with the techniques and skilful fighters,' he tells me. 'But here in North America, even with MMA and UFC, they want to go for the win in thirty seconds. There's a missing philosophy – you learn, you prepare, you train for months before you go to the ring. But then you only spend thirty seconds to win!' In Muay Thai, he continues passionately, 'we want to, number one, testify to our skill, and, number two, our power, and number three, our technique to build the next levels.'

It is an outlook that has resonated with so many of his students. I spoke with Danny Cabrera, founder of the WOLF Athletic Academy, a Muay Thai gym in Toronto. Cabrera is the kind of guy you can have a few beers with, but he is also a lifelong lover of martial arts. He knows exactly what Suchart's modus operandi is. 'He believes in authentic traditional Muay Thai, Thai people, Thai culture, Thai spirituality, Thai technique. That's it,' says Cabrera, who also trains his students in Brazilian jiu-jitsu, a martial art that is very focused on ground fighting and submission holds. If you want to train someone in Muay Thai, he says, don't water it down with another martial art.

In North America, however, fight culture has a hard time with that concept, Cabrera adds. 'That's the reason why a lot of our clubs have kept away [from teaching Muay Thai],' he says. Muay Thai, tactically but also culturally, is a different beast altogether.

'Like, even for me, as a gym owner here, I don't really get too many MMA guys. They're different, you know – it's a different mentality,' Cabrera explains. 'They're both vicious sports, but the MMA mentality is a little bit like, "Hey, I want to spar, bro, like, where can I bang?" And that's not how you talk when you're in front of Muay Thai krus. They teach a beautiful Muay Thai with tradition and culture and heritage."

One notable local kru is Clifton Brown, a Jamaican-born fighter who became the first Canadian to hold the world championship crown in Muay Thai. He has a long winning record, coaches the first Canadian national Muay Thai team, and will likely coach Team Canada in the 2024 Olympics.

Clifton got his start in Toronto, and Suchart was his first coach. Theirs is a long-time friendship that Clifton treasures. Like most fighters, Clifton loves Western forms of fight sports – kickboxing, UFC, Bellator, and other MMA promotions. He is also a big fan of Western boxing, and admired Mike Tyson, not for his out-of-ring life, which has been toxic and damaging, but for his impact on heavyweight boxing culture.

Tyson, in fact, inspired Cabrera to get involved in fighting. 'It was the first bug that bit me, and I've never gotten over it,' he says. 'I love Muay Thai. Muay Thai is in my blood, but there's something about the "sweet science" that cannot be beat. It's beautiful.'

Suchart himself loves fight sports and watches MMA and other competitions pretty closely. But he has chosen to stick to his discipline. 'When you go to Thailand, and if you go to a Muay Thai camp, it's intertwined,' he says. 'When you see pre-fight dances, and see the fighters wear ceremonial garb, you're recognizing how greatly integrated Muay Thai is with the larger culture. Everything is linked to spirituality. So if you're a hard-core atheist, and may not like anything, it's not for you, because they intertwine it 100 per cent.'

• • •

After years of developing gyms, training athletes, and advocating for his sport, Suchart is closing in on the final bell: full legitimacy for a sport that is more than just a sport. In December 2016, the International Federation of Muaythai Associations (IFMA) – in effect, the sport itself – was invited to join the Association of International Olympic Committee-Recognized Sports Federations (ARISF). It was a big step. The IFMA had lobbied the International Olympic Committee for decades to gain acceptance and, therefore, a chance to see Muay Thai acknowledged as an Olympic sport. Admission to the ARISF meant Muay Thai would become eligible for IOC development funding.

Sports that are selected to be in the Olympics usually come from within the ARISF membership. The most recent sports include breakdancing, which is going to be in the Olympics in 2024.

Suchart helped set in motion the IFMA's efforts to gain that acceptance. Since the days when few had even heard of Muay Thai, so much has changed, thanks to his teaching and the growing ranks of krus who graduate from his school. His leadership in

North American Muay Thai, along with the efforts of other advocates, put the sport on the IOC's radar.

'That is my goal, you know,' says Suchart. 'Now we got a step already announced by the European Union. We are in the European Championship. We have one more inch. One more inch and we're going to be in the Olympics, you know? It's so close right now.'

One more inch.

In the summer of 2021, during the Tokyo Games, the IOC announced that Muay Thai, along with kickboxing and Sambo, was given formal status and would be present in the 2024 games.

The long-sought moment caused Suchart to offer some reflections on his Facebook page.

> This is one part of my legacy ... students who became fighters, who I have taught from the start, to become champions. Many of these Champions have gone on to do great things for themselves and for the sport of Muay Thai. Some have opened their own schools and are now training their own students, who are now my grand-students.
>
> Some continue to fight at the international level and continue to show the world their strength, power, and skill. Others have moved around the world and continue to teach and share Muay Thai while pursuing other successful careers. This is part of my legacy – to leave a positive mark on the lives of people through Muay Thai. There is another chapter of my life about to start, one that includes continuing to support Krus, and students of Muay Thai around the world and to pursue the development of the Sport by training athletes for the Olympics. I believe.

16

THE DEATH AND REBIRTH
OF THE WOLFPACK

When I set out to write this book, the saga of the Toronto Wolfpack, the city's first professional rugby team, seemed pretty cut and dried. Never a grassroots operation, the owners wanted to grow a business. They saw an opening in the market and worked tirelessly to bring fans and the local community into the fold, to build a connection that any sports club should have, in my opinion.

The Wolfpack's backers reached a goal, competing in the United Kingdom–based Super League, the world's pre-eminent rugby organization. It was an audacious goal for a franchise that seemed to come out of nowhere in 2017, billing itself as the first 'transatlantic professional sports team.' David Argyle, an Australian who made his fortune in mining, put up the financing – almost $400,000 – to the Rugby Football League. The squad aggressively recruited experienced pros to serve during the team's early years, and then began competing in the third-tier Kingstone Press League 1, which includes teams from England, Wales, and France. Argyle said the Wolfpack would pay the travel and housing expenses for visiting teams until it joined the Super League.

The club made a deal with the City of Toronto to use Allan A. Lamport Stadium, a throwback arena in Liberty Village that's straight out of the seventies. The place is named for former mayor Allan Lamport, who famously fought the blue laws, which banned commercial activity on Sundays but had no problems with sporting events on that day.

With co-founder Eric Perez, Argyle reportedly put in millions of his own money to ensure the team would keep climbing the promotion ladder that led to the Super League. The Wolfpack even documented its inaugural season with a web series entitled, perhaps ominously, *Last Tackle: Inside the Toronto Wolfpack*. Argyle wanted his squad to be competitive and visible from day one.

But this story isn't just about a rich man throwing money at a vanity project. The Wolfpack's success had to be fuelled by a community of fans that did not exist before the team's arrival. To build the kind of loyalty that can sustain a pro team, a large group of people needed to keep coming out to games, and that would take a lot of work.

In an interview in 2019, Jon Pallett, the Wolfpack's then Vice President, Commercial, and a veteran of Welsh rugby, tells me the team was negotiating a long-term lease that would make Lamport Stadium 'home.' 'We will be looking to make various improvements to the stadium to allow us to host games. So a bit of a facelift on the stadium, things like the electrics and the power, but also some of the things about the changing rooms and the field of play and all of this stuff,' he says. To generate some good faith, the team forged relationships with the local BIA, the local councillor, the local residents' association, and a local charity. But to make the math work, the Pack would have to get at least 100,000 fans through the gates for the 2020 season. The owners had a ten-year plan, with a Super League victory at the other end.

And then the whole enterprise got tackled by the pandemic.

• • •

When it comes to professional sports, Toronto has been fertile ground for upstart franchises, including the Blue Jays, the Raptors, and the Toronto FC. But what you may not know is that Toronto is also the graveyard for more professional teams than you might guess. My former *Toronto Star* colleague, Sean Fitz-Gerald, found ten, including the storied Maple Leafs baseball team, the Toronto

Toros of the short-lived World Hockey Association, and a football franchise called the Toronto Phantoms. The Wolfpack figured they could dodge the bullets that felled these other teams.

Rugby is a bit like football without the gear, and with a lot more jargon. Have you ever watched a tackled player create a 'ruck'? Or seen a squad weave, arm in arm, as they form a scrum and work to regain possession of the leathery oblong ball? As it turns out, many Torontonians know all about this sport, which has a healthy but cult-like following in the GTA.

I've covered rugby here for a while, and there is a tremendous community around the sport – a fact that the Wolfpack owners must have known. For years, I covered the Balmy Beach Rugby Club, based in the Beaches. Its history tracks back generations and has spawned Olympians and World Cup–calibre players – women and men alike.

The club is based at the foot of Beech Avenue and plays out of Tubs & Gee Gage Rugby Field in Ashbridges Bay Park. Founded in 1955, it programs rugby for hundreds of kids, as well as senior men's and women's squads. There are others of similar vintage: the Toronto Scottish Rugby Football Club and the Ajax Wanderers Rugby Club, both with loyal followings and deep ties to their communities. In the GTA, the centre of the rugby universe is Fletcher's Fields in Markham, home base to many other local rugby clubs.

Rugby groups have worked to be more inclusive of late, creating spaces for the marginalized. Some school programs, like one at Oakwood Collegiate, have done a great job of providing different sports experiences for students. Oakwood allowed students of colour to compete in a sport that has been, to be honest, mostly white and male.

Then there's the Muddy York RFC. Established in 2003, Muddy York provides rugby for the LGBTQ2S+ community and friends. The club really caught my attention when it posted a YouTube video entitled *The Gay Who Wasn't Gay Enough*. In it, a man named Richard explains how, after coming out, he discovered he was more in his element on a rugby pitch than in any other context. 'Gay men, playing rugby?' he jokes. 'I mean, what's gay about rugby? What I found on that field was a confidence, a brotherhood. The ability to challenge my limits and tackle my fears. Did I know anything about the sport? No. Could I break something? Sure, namely a stereotype or two. Did I want a piece of that? You bet.'

As its advocacy efforts show, Muddy York is about more than rugby. The club's mission is also to use sports to confront depression and other mental health issues among LGBTQ2S+ youth. (U.S. research has shown that LGBTQ youth who are involved in sports do better in school and are less prone to depression or suicide than those who don't play.) The club now does coed training for newbies and partners with other GTA rugby clubs. Its vision is to 'radically change the way we think of, join in, and enjoy sports, leading to a more inclusive society,' as the club says in its newsletter.

I could go on about the richness and depth of the GTA's rugby community, and its fight to create a better world for all sorts of players. Which makes the story about the fate of the Wolfpack all the more interesting. And sad, if you really think about it.

• • •

In 2019, Wolfpack owner David Argyle made a racist comment about Jose Kenga, a Congolese man who played for an opposing team. He soon quit as chair and chief executive of the club. He declined to speak to me for this book.

But then the pandemic overshadowed the controversy, halting whatever momentum the team had built up. The players literally couldn't fly and compete with clubs overseas without taking a large hit financially. They couldn't generate ticket, merchandise, or concession revenue. And the team's players weren't allowed to collect furlough supports from either the United Kingdom or the Canadian government.

Finally, and this one slays me, the Wolfpack couldn't share in the Super League's television revenues, which is mind-boggling given how they'd clawed their way up to the top-flight division after only a few years. Throughout this whole saga, I was in touch with Bob Hunter, the Wolfpack's CEO and chair. At the time, we were both waiting on the Super League's decision on whether or not to re-admit the Wolfpack into the league. They had played matches in Manchester, but only got a few in before COVID shut everything down.

Hunter is well-known in Toronto sports circles – a former executive with Maple Leaf Sports & Entertainment. He seemed fairly calm, not at all panicked that the club was in limbo. 'Part of our big challenge is how to grow and develop the sport at the youth level,' he tells me. 'It's just not as mainstream. There are pockets of rugby around the country, but those are very specific.' Many are tied to private schools.

Yet he feels that, in Toronto, the sport could actually grow beyond the bubbles of private schools and private clubs. 'I mean, it's just why Toronto FC have done so well over the years: a lot of people play soccer. Can rugby ever be mainstream? No, but I think it can have a decent fan base to support this sport.'

When the Pack finally ran out of gas, it managed to pay off its players and staff, but the team couldn't finish the 2020 season. In August 2020, Argyle, who estimates his ownership group invested $30 million into the team with little or no return, stepped aside. Carlo LiVolsi, a Canadian businessman and former associate of Argyle's, became the new owner and promised to underwrite the team's losses – to the tune of millions of pounds. Super League officials didn't buy it and pulled the plug.

As the BBC reported, 'A committee appointed by Super League to investigate Toronto's proposal to return to the competition has strongly recommended that they should be denied readmission – concluding, amongst other things, that LiVolsi does not provide sufficient evidence of long-term funding for the club.'

The team eventually resurfaced in 2021 as a member of the newly formed North American Rugby League, whose first season begins in 2022. Looking back, the twists and turns of the Wolfpack story are dizzying. As a Canadian Press sports columnist pointed out, the team's central gambit – to play in a league that is primarily British – amounted to a fool's errand. 'Thanks to the powers that be in [the] English rugby league, the Wolfpack were built on a rotten foundation,' he wrote. 'Expansion to North America was fine as long as the U.K. contingent didn't have to pay for it.'

Yet this melodrama made me realize something else, which is that rebuilding the city's spirit after the pandemic is going to be the most challenging task of our lifetime.

17

A CITY WITHOUT SPORT

Jeff Chung won't stop teaching nine-man volleyball to his children and promoting a game played in Kensington Market to the Chinese communities around the region. Lisa Grogan-Green and Lauren Wolman don't intend to stop helping marginalized communities access team sports like cricket, so no kids are left behind. Lee Anna Osei won't stop trying to build equity into Canadian basketball by channelling her hometown spirit into coaching circles from coast to coast.

And Lali Toor won't sideline his efforts to make hockey look more like Toronto, from the top professional ranks to the communities he walks through each day, and not just on concrete surfaces with rubber balls, but also on the ice.

Creating a city that reflects its residents is, and will always be, in the hands of the communities and people who live it and shape it. And there are so many individuals and leaders, like these men and women, who are prepared to do this work. But a virus turned their goal into a death match, changing how we envision Toronto's future.

• • •

When COVID-19 took hold in our communities in March 2020, public health agencies and governments set in motion one of the most dramatic movements in recent memory: they required most of us to stay home. People were restricted from public spaces.

Large gatherings were banned. Arenas and community centres closed. A great quiet came down on our communities. As essential workers continued to travel to long-term care homes, supermarkets, and other critical spaces, the privileged, including myself, mainly worked from home. The virus picked off the elderly, the poor, and communities of colour. It exposed how we live and work. It also revealed how we play, and what we lose when we have to stop.

The unfortunate truth is that even before the pandemic struck, we had already begun to stop playing. It's a story Kristina Leis, who was raised in the Lawrence Park neighbourhood of Toronto, knows very well. A teacher, she grew up involved in sports and athletics. 'Throughout my childhood, I was playing soccer and in leagues consistently,' she tells me. 'I still have one of my trophies from when I was nine!'

Lawrence Park is upper middle class and, honestly, a bit WASPY. But it's a community dedicated to sports. Sporting Life's 10K, one of the city's popular road races, traditionally started there. Lawrence Park Collegiate has graduated some of the city's more successful amateur athletes, in sports like tennis, hockey, cross-country, and track. As a sports reporter, I covered Lawrence Park football quite closely. The Panthers compete fairly well with the best in the city and province. Outside the school, you can find a vibrant local football program, the Metro Toronto Wildcats, which has produced hundreds of graduates, including one of my favourite Argos, Matt Black. It's a tight-knit community, and the football club is seen as one model for community-building.

Leis loves the city when sports take centre stage. She has fond memories of the 2006 World Cup, when St. Clair West flooded with hundreds of thousands of fans of Azzurri, the Italian champions. For all that, she found herself playing less as she grew older. After finishing her master's degree, she took up yoga as part of a healing process and then began kicking around the soccer ball again. 'I ended up joining a league in Toronto,' she says, referring to the Toronto Sport & Social Club, which enrols thousands of adults in activities from basketball and soccer to tennis and golf. 'I'd never played recreationally before.'

Her story is not unfamiliar. For many women, accessing recreation is still a difficult task for a litany of reasons – lack of inclusive opportunities, financial and social barriers, and implicit and explicit gender discrimination. These are long-standing problems, and the trends are not going in the right direction.

According to a 2020 study by Canadian Women and Sport, a sports advocacy organization, one in three girls drop out of sports during adolescence. By comparison, one in ten boys drop out at that age. 'In 1992,' CTV News reported of the findings, 'just over half of women aged fifteen or older were participating in sport. That dropped to 35 per cent by 2010. Only 18 per cent of women aged sixteen to sixty-three are currently involved in sport. Among the barriers that affected girls' continuation in sport, one in three listed low confidence, negative body image, perceived lack of skill, or poor perceptions of belonging and feeling unwelcome.'

Leis has long believed that active living was an aspect of her life that she wanted to restore and nourish. When the pandemic hit, her regular games disappeared in favour of group chats on Zoom with her teammates. 'Everyone is so antsy because we are used to getting together every Sunday or every Saturday for a game,' she said.

The sense of loss was strong, and extended beyond her sense of physical fitness. 'You lose that momentum of going out and having something to do; you lose that social aspect, that team aspect,' she says. 'Going out and doing these things allows you to connect with yourself on a deeper level – like I hit that goal and that accomplishment – and then having that trust in yourself to follow through.'

The loss of activity and all that comes with it prompted Leis and many others to realize how they'd taken for granted those opportunities to participate in sports. And the pandemic revealed something else that's key to this story: that Toronto has a crisis of public space.

The communities whose residents were most likely to fall ill or die were also the most likely to lose access to the tools they needed to live, such as having access to recreational facilities, public parks, and the like. The 2020 ParticipACTION report card made that loss clear: children and youth were given a D-plus for overall physical activity and a D-plus for sedentary behaviours. The non-profit also found that only 39 per cent of children (aged five to eleven) and youths (twelve to seventeen) were meeting national guidelines of sixty minutes of moderate to vigorous physical activity per day.

As *Globe and Mail* reporter Dakshana Bascaramurty noted in a 2020 story on the class and race implications of COVID-19 restrictions on leisure, 'Service providers and those who research the socio-cultural dimensions of sport stress that the impact goes far beyond mere restlessness – there could be serious long-term effects on mental health and safety and a lost sense of community that should be weighed against the COVID-19 risk.' The story pointed out that golf courses and tennis courts reopened more quickly than basketball courts and playgrounds, underscoring issues of equity.

The policing of certain spaces deepened these divisions. The City of Toronto imposed fines totalling $400,000 to people contravening social distancing rules, and half were for use of park amenities, such as exercise equipment, sports fields, or basketball courts, including makeshift ones created in parking lots. The concern among people of colour, Bascaramurty wrote, is whether there are safe spaces at all.

Other experts agreed. A University of Toronto research team found that the pandemic 'exposed the underfunding and neglect of physical education and [community sport] … with a likely severe impact on mental health and general well-being.' The study, which described community sport as a 'significant' source of resilience, also warned that the pandemic would exacerbate the already lower participation of girls and women.

But the U of T team also talked about a silver lining:

Many local governments and sports organizations developed innovative approaches to the changed circumstances the virus necessitated, creating programming that could be delivered online and by traditional media such as radio and loudspeakers; modifying and creating new activities appropriate to restricted environments; closing streets and opening new bike lanes to enable physically distanced walking, running, and cycling; and working with public health experts to develop safe 'return to play' guidelines.

• • •

Urban cycling may be one of the pandemic's most far-reaching legacies. New York City implemented new and temporary bike lanes from Broadway to Queens, from Midtown Manhattan to Harlem. Paris installed 'corona cycleways' along fifty kilometres of once car-choked streets. Many cities were encouraging people to ride as a way to avoid crowding on public transit. 'Authorities say the need for social distancing leaves them little choice,' the New York Times reported.

Bike lanes were the easy pivot in Canada, too. In June 2020, CBC reported that 'Vancouver, Victoria, Calgary, Winnipeg, Ottawa, Kitchener, Montreal, and Moncton all extended their cycling networks,' citing a report from Vélo Canada Bikes, a bicycle advocacy group.

Such initiatives are unquestionably popular. The David Suzuki Foundation, in a September 2020 poll, found that 84 per cent of Torontonians wanted the city to be doing more to make their streets safer, and bike lanes make a big difference. But, despite reports that residents are biking for the first time and using bike lanes more than ever, council may yet reverse these moves, scaling back on what's been built or pausing future expansion.

Some critics see bike lanes as an impediment. One city councillor, Stephen Holyday, doubts their long-term viability and warns about the risks of building new lanes.

'Once they're installed they're very hard to remove, so we have to be very, very careful.'

But we have to look at the bike-lane story in a broader context. The pandemic revealed not only the need for public space, but the importance of animating and improving it to provide benefits for all those who don't have the means to pay for recreation, activity, and community sports.

The U of T team went further, urging local governments to develop pandemic-ready strategies for community sports for development, boost investments in sport as a preventative health approach, apply a gender equity lens, and recognize physical activity as an essential component of population health. One particular recommendation fired up a bunch of synapses for me: 'Ensure as much as possible that the public space innovations introduced in urban areas during COVID-19, such as the street closures and additional bike lanes that have enabled safe walking, running, and cycling, are made permanent.' After all, Toronto's livability is directly linked to its walkability and accessibility.

• • •

Because the pandemic has forced us to make connections between public space, equity, health, and participation in community sports, I found myself thinking of some conversations I had in 2019 with officials at the Aspen Institute, a non-partisan think tank based in Washington, D.C. It had pivoted to sports in a big way the year before, becoming co-founder of Project Play, an initiative founded by the late NBA superstar Kobe Bryant and American Olympian Allyson Felix.

When I interview Jon Solomon, who heads Aspen's Sports & Society Program, he poses what is, in hindsight, a highly prescient question. 'How can sport be used to serve the public interest?' he wonders. 'It's less about "How do we create the greatest athletes? How do we win? How do we make money? How do we succeed, thrive?" If we're redefining what success looks like, how do we create athletes for life?'

Project Play, he continues, 'is an initiative where we're trying to increase youth sports participation, and build healthy communities through physical activity and having kids be more physically active.'

Bryant, before his tragic death, had plenty to say about this topic. 'Sport is not some extracurricular add-on to American life,' he observed at the 2018 Project Play Summit. 'It's not a sideshow to the political and the economic questions that dominate policy discussions. This is nation-building.'

He continued: 'I feel like most of the time, as adults, we overcomplicate things and emotionally we tend to get in our own way a lot.' Bryant noted that adults should 'get out of the way' and allow children to enjoy less-structured sports and build up their imaginations and ambitions.

These outlooks take on even more importance as we try to figure out what 'return to play' looks like. When I check in on Aspen's Project Play Summit in 2020, Tom Farrey, the institute's executive director of its Sports & Society Program, acknowledges just how massive this project has become. 'The long-term challenge of recovering from COVID-19 will be even more difficult than the Great Recession,' he predicts. 'There are both financial and health factors to return to play.'

We face the very same issues in Toronto. However, the solutions, which have everything to do with the future growth of the region itself, should be custom-built for the city and its residents.

18

REBOUND

Greater Toronto's future includes growth, and a lot of it. In 2019, the City of Toronto grew by about 46,000 people, and the population of the wider Greater Golden Horseshoe region, which takes in everything from Peterborough to Fort Erie to Waterloo, is expected to swell from its current 9 million to 13.5 million by 2041. The Ontario government describes the region as one of North America's fastest growing.

Because the city ranks so high in global livability rankings, people want to come here to live and work. In 2020, we had more cranes in the sky – 121, give or take – than any other North American city. As of early 2019, there were over seventy thousand new condo units under construction in the GTA. Residential real estate is prohibitively costly. Land is expensive. Opportunities for affordable housing have dried up. Space is scarce, and it's in demand.

So one specific question about Toronto's future is about its public spaces and recreational amenities. At the moment, parks account for 13 per cent, or eight thousand hectares, of the City of Toronto, although many – 39 per cent – are small. The city itself admits that population growth will put a squeeze on our parks and ravines unless more space is found. The looming scarcity of parkland, in my assessment, will most affect communities of colour, immigrant communities, and high-density neighbourhoods.

'Without public spaces, you really lose out on the community benefits that come with it,' says Madeline Ashby, a Toronto futurist. 'The fight to get public space and to keep space public is a fight that is going on in cities everywhere right now.' She worries about a city where more and more space will become private, including spaces for recreation or sports, like gyms. 'When we privatize space, we also privatize rules,' she observes. 'When we cut off public space, we're not just cutting out the opportunities for cardiovascular health, but also the opportunities for mental health. By limiting access, we are determining who gets to be healthy.'

These concerns became especially relevant during the pandemic, when so many people lost access to public space. The health crisis may have accelerated the arrival of a tipping point in terms of how the city will function in the future. 'You have to face these things in a different way,' Ashby says. 'A crisis like the pandemic does sort of initiate that kind of thinking. "Oh, the world as we knew it is going to be different. The world as we knew it is over."' The question then is, what's next? What will Toronto actually become? When so many of us work and access resources primarily online, what will it actually mean to live in a certain place? And where do sports and physical activity, and the community they create, fit into the picture?

• • •

This debate is not about professional leagues, TV deals, or star players, with all the emphasis on business and performance. The pandemic certainly revealed the vulnerability of a multi-billion-dollar industry. From the moment on March 11, 2020, when NBA forward Rudy Gobert tested positive for the coronavirus – causing the NBA and every other major sports league to postpone games and retreat into bubbles – to the empty stands at the Tokyo Olympics in the summer of 2021, high-level sports hasn't encountered such intense disruption since the World War II.

The disruption the pandemic caused gives us the opportunity to rethink cities and neighbourhoods, to imagine a new ideal. One day, years from now, this ideal city will have equipped itself and its citizens with the tools to resist hardship, to encourage

Emijah, who lives in the Malvern neighbourhood in Scarborough, took part in the At Home, In the Game *art project. He was one of twelve kids to take part.*
(Courtesy of Ebti Nabag)

local engagement, and, frankly, to make our sporting lives more connected, competitive, and fun.

In that city, we will have built up a portfolio of public spaces that fill the gaps that currently exist. Those spaces will come to be through a rethinking of public and private property by policymakers. The reclamation of distressed sites, like brownfields and unused lots, are part of the growing portfolios of land trusts and co-operative properties that are proliferating across the city. Many have been set aside for affordable housing, but surplus lots in that future city will also be used for sports, for activities, for connecting with our neighbours.

On several of those reclaimed lands in this dream city will be multi-sport facilities. Some of them, like Go Green Youth Centre, already exist. Toronto's Port Lands and parts of Downsview Park (which will be redeveloped in the 2020s) could also have smartly designed multi-sport spaces.

In this future city, stadium and facility technologies will make it possible to accommodate multiple large-field sports – soccer, rugby, football – into the same location. Hockey rinks won't quite look the same, because these ice rinks and sheets will also accommodate non-ice activities – with a technology similar to that in use at the Scotiabank Arena. Taking cues from technologies developed by the Atlanta Falcons (which built Mercedes-Benz Stadium in the 2010s), these large facilities will be environmentally sustainable with small ecological footprints – water runoff mitigation systems, energy-efficient lighting, and connections to local food production. They will also be well integrated into public transit and bike infrastructure, encouraging many of us to use alternate forms of transport to attend and engage in these spaces.

Technology aside, these facilities and these new community centres, are blank canvases; they're places where new or emerging sports can be practised, reflecting the desires of newcomers and immigrants. Rugby and cricket leagues will have caught on in a way that rivals basketball's growth in Toronto in the 1990s and 2000s.

Besides sports, such facilities will also be hubs for social services for newcomers and immigrants. Supports for girls, racialized kids, the disabled, and LGBTQ2S+ people fill the landscape and engage with each other as they fight against discrimination. Organizing and networking will occur in these places. Local democracy will redefine how we approach sports by capturing and fostering what sports is about: people, connection, and rallying together to solve our collective problems.

How will these places get built? We will pay for them. In fact, we will have found a way to subsidize new infrastructure in the old-fashioned way: wealthier people will see the dividends in investing locally, pay their fair share in taxes, and give their time and money to create facilities that reflect current needs and future desires. We will build these places using better data and analysis.

Everything I just mentioned could make a huge difference, but these ideas will be difficult to execute and achieve. Yet they can happen if communities – parents, of course, but also educators and schools, sports clubs and community groups – speak up and advocate effectively.

It must begin with parents. They get active as coaches and stewards of sports in their communities, creating new ways for kids to play. The basketball movement began this way, but I feel like it's an easy approach to promote other sports. On top of their involvement, parents must make sports about having fun, aligning health and well-being, and introducing high-performance options when these young athletes are ready (e.g., at age thirteen, as in Norway, which has mandated youth programming). We should develop mentorship opportunities for girls, racialized youth, and teenagers. We should listen to the late Kobe Bryant but also listen to what kids want and need for their own growth. It's not just about 'build it and they will come.'

In our communities, business improvement associations and residents' and tenants' groups must work to make their open spaces more active and inclusive. As happened in the pandemic, BIAS can promote more creative uses for their streetscapes, more than just pedestrian events and food festivals. Residents' associations, meanwhile, should be lobbying park staff for broader use of local park spaces, encouraging sports events and the like.

If schools, educators, parents, and kids begin to organize, they will make the case for further investment. These groups can promote a Charter for Children's Rights in Sport (also originally a European idea) that defines kids' needs and lays out strategies for active living, including standards for activity. We must enhance long-term development plans and models in Canada, recalibrating what we need to get the nation on its feet. We can't design sports participation solely to produce athletes to send to the Olympics. We need more than that from sports, for our own health and happiness.

The federal and provincial governments should implement their own Charters for Youth Participation, and not ignore what is happening in our communities. Frankly, it is a non-partisan win – everyone benefits from rapidly growing use of public spaces.

With underpinning principles and evidence in place, governments can direct monies from single-game sports betting (which became legal in Canada in 2021) and gambling to youth sports and sports infrastructure.

We can rally because the pandemic was a wake-up call – we see how it adversely affected our lives, and especially what it has done to our children. We need to create solutions where they will make a difference: in our neighbourhoods and communities.

To me, sports in the city is something we invest in physically and emotionally. It is organized and developed collectively in the spaces we hold dear. Sports is an extension of ourselves – if we choose to extend ourselves that way. In Toronto, it's also something more: part of the spirit of this place. It's a result of the work communities have done to keep people together, for decades – cohesive, communicative, and playful communities. It's not a trait, but rather the character of how we live together. For all those reasons, we mourned its loss during the long months of lockdown.

Maybe that's why private arenas, sitting empty, became spaces to serve during the pandemic. Some became kitchens and distribution networks for meals for front-line health-care workers and the residents of shelters. Others, like Sacramento's Sleep Train Arena, turned into makeshift field hospitals, COVID testing facilities, voting stations, and venues for mass vaccination drives, as happened at the Scotiabank Arena.

Sports, in other words, didn't stick to sports. These organizations became civic partners. And, pushed by disaster, a rethink became a possibility – a window on how we can create a more inclusive culture of sports in the future.

The arenas and the pro teams will survive. But what happens to local leagues, or people who play recreationally but depend on the locker rooms that became dangerous and may remain restricted until the pandemic subsides? 'Sport itself is just going to have to either be on hold, or figure out a way that is safer for athletes to do what it is that they have to do,' Ashby says when we speak in 2020. 'Gyms are a very dangerous place right now.' Those risks could end sports as we know them.

On the other hand, our pandemic-prompted rethink of our public and recreational spaces should bring renewed attention to good ideas that have already germinated, such as the flexible multi-use facilities at Go Green. These facilities can solve a combination of problems – how we accommodate diverse social interests, how we conceptualize large public spaces, and how we design facilities that better reflect local needs. But we have some work to do if we want to create something truly intersectional, spaces that look like the city that surrounds them.

Lauren Wolman, who advocated for Go Green, says communities and sports organizations need to pay particular attention to gender as they plan for the return to play. Girls, she cautions, may never come back: 'A girl is scared to even get on the pitch or the basketball court in the first place because she's culturally, socially, not the dominant group there and she messes up.'

Post-pandemic community sports programming, Wolman says, will need to involve more mentorship as well as messaging that girls should be claiming space on fields, pitches, and arenas. That kind of programming, she adds, must also be financially sustainable. Governments need to expand the ways in which they fund local sports and fitness projects and guide them at different stages of their growth. Such funding doesn't exist now. In fact, in the crisis atmosphere that prevailed during the pandemic, sports projects were not at the top of the list of spending priorities.

Ashby also observed that vulnerable communities are accustomed to contending with hardship and uncertainty, so this is nothing new. 'The sense of insecurity and uncertainty and unpredictability,' she says, 'is something that populations of colour, people in poverty, immigrants, trans kids, homeless people go through on a daily basis.' But, she adds, the pandemic affected everyone in some way. 'It forced its way into the suburbs, right?' Even the privileged lost access to sports facilities. Which means that just about everyone should now be eager to fight for those spaces.

For that reason, it has caused us to look at each other's lives. The hardships faced by front-line workers should make privileged communities feel uncomfortable. Those revelations can give rise to calls to action. And when it comes to the sports and games we play, maybe we can realize that we share a mindset about their importance that extends across social divides.

However, an inclusive sporting future means fighting for the quality and quantity of public spaces, understanding how the city works, finding new sources of revenue, and recognizing how different people live. To build the city we want, we'll need to spend time reckoning with ourselves.

My hope is that the pandemic has given everyone a chance to envision a future that works not just for themselves, but for people they don't know, too. We don't need to debate the importance of equity, safe spaces, and the case for working together. These are the essential traits of the imperfect puzzle that is the city. Supporting our communities and neighbours – listening to their pain, their experiences of racism or poverty – and then acting to eliminate that pain: this is what we need to do as a city.

Sports will be a crucial piece of this process. These pastimes show that people who don't know each other can come together to pursue a common goal. Everyone, from hijab-wearing ballers to disabled athletes, LGBTQ2S+ rugby players, and seniors practising Tai Chi, should have a chance to play. It is essential to living in the city.

Whenever I'm in Parkdale, visiting family and friends, I always find my way back to the Masaryk-Cowan Community Recreation Centre. I don't work out there much anymore. But for me, this place is where the city is most alive. One day, after the pandemic recedes, the Lungta basketball tournament will be back on.

I fully expect a packed house.

ACKNOWLEDGEMENTS

When I earned an opportunity to write about sports for Coach House Books, I wanted to do something that got to the core of what sports is and can be, and how we can use that knowledge to make us better thinkers – about sports, about cities, about history, and especially about the future. This kind of layered, nuanced writing came with the patience, guidance, and support of the staff of Coach House Books. I'm grateful for Alana Wilcox's editorial leadership and John Lorinc's critical feedback. They gave me carte blanche to go in any direction I chose. I think what you have read is a reflection of thoughtful help and encouragement. To produce one of the very few sports-focused books for this publisher is an honour and privilege that I do not take lightly.

My family, friends, and colleagues have been cheerleaders of my project since I began. There were many inspirations for this book, but my youngest brother, Andrew, and his future as a basketball player sparked my curious journey. Thank you, Drew, for your indirect but profound impact on me and this book. My wife, Hilary, nurtured my passion for this project – and motivated me to the end. My parents, Consuela and Terrence, have been gushing with excitement over *Rebound*'s arrival. My friends have been nothing but encouraging. I'm lucky to have them all in my corner. Thank you, everyone.

I wouldn't be in a position to tell these kinds of sports stories without the trust and enthusiasm of sportswriters and editors I've worked with over the years: Adrian Bradbury, Meg Campbell, Emina Gamulin, Shawn Micallef, Gordon Cameron, and Eric McMillan were all early voices in my development as a journalist. They put me on beats that explored sports at a grassroots level. Denise Balkissoon, Matthew Blackett, and Marc Glassman gave me a chance to explore stories that were not being told – sports stories, but also narratives about the future, race, history, and urban affairs. I thank them all eternally for giving me a chance to try new things, but also to deliver quality news and feature writing that I could be proud of.

Rebound, above all, is an exploration of our modern city and how it can change. My storytelling here, and our actions as a city, take place on Indigenous land – the traditional territory of many nations, including the Mississaugas of the Credit, the Anishnabeg, the Chippewa, the Haudenosaunee, and the Wendat peoples, and now home to many diverse First Nations, Inuit, and Métis peoples. Keeping this in mind has helped me to reflect and consider how to make a difference, how these communities – but also many other marginalized communities – can empower themselves to create a better city. I would hope that all audiences can take away something from Rebound and carry forward the conversation. This book is not the final word, nor even the first word, but another starting point in the conversation, as we continuously and collectively work toward a better life.

Some of this book was built on the previous research and stories (close to two decades worth) about numerous GTA-based sports organizations, people, and places – and not just my own work. They are too many to name, but I am grateful to these story subjects, from all walks of life, who trusted and shared their stories with me. They all encompass some small part of the grander puzzle that is this city. Cities are tremendous riddles, created by colonization and also zones of struggle and hope. I say this without hesitation – these people, places, and things make the city what it is. They make sports beyond fitness and recreation, so it becomes a space to organize and socialize and unite for a common cause. Sport moves the needle on how the city grows. As you navigate and think about this city, I hope you think about the stories in Rebound, but also those of your neighbours. Endeavour to know more about your fellow neighbours and do things to make this place more livable for everyone.

The Rebound story began with an ending – the last days of Eastern Commerce – and the fruitful beginnings it created. Lou Sialtsis, Kevin Jeffers, and Kareem Griffin were gateways to a better understanding of the world of high-performance basketball in this city, but their work is part of a larger community of men and women, girls and boys, who created an unprecedented movement in the GTA. I thank these three individuals for the beginning of this sub-journey in the book. Sami Hill, Lee Anna Osei, Shane Stirling, Luke Galati, Ebti Nabag, and Chris Penrose were also very open and sharing of their stories, and I thank them for helping me deliver a book I can be proud of.

Rebound houses a small sampling of Vaughan, Ontario's basketball story. The story didn't begin with coaches Gus Gymnopoulos and Dwayne Sybliss, but they are deeply supportive of the students in their care. They understand the power of sports within the realm of education, and I wish them many successes in their passions. And I thank them for talking to me for this book.

(And it must be said: basketball is the official sport of the City of Toronto. It's not a fad and it's not going anywhere. I'm happy to see marginalized communities equip themselves as they educate and mould generations of boys and girls.)

Eliminating racism and discrimination in all its forms – whether it be Islamophobia, anti-LGBT2S+, ableist, and ageist – can't be accomplished by just some people. It is a collective burden we all must confront, and I hope the stories shared in *Rebound* have given you some indication of the work being done in multiple platforms and spaces among Torontonians. I would like to thank Jaskaran Singh Sandhu, Lali Toor, and Jaspaul Singh for communicating how South Asian communities are addressing discrimination in their circles. Courtney Szto is a leader – someone who is thoughtful and passionate about hockey communities near and far – and I thank her for sharing her journey as a sports researcher. Follow her work and support it. Karl Subban was so understanding and insightful about hockey, family, and education. I would like to thank him, and his *How We Did It* co-author Scott Colby, for making sure Karl's story formed a small part of *Rebound*.

The nine-man volleyball community shared a moment in time, but their story isn't defined by that moment. They are a community that celebrates sports as a community builder – where players can fully be themselves with people they trust and can connect with each other on a deeper level. I would like to thank Hannah Sung, who put nine-man on my radar, and for introducing me to players and thinkers. Yuka Nakamura shared her incredible work and gave me insight I didn't previously understand. Thank you, Yuka. To Ursula Liang, an incredible filmmaker and journalist, thank you for your insights – even if we couldn't connect on the record for this book. Jeff Chung, thank you for sharing your story with me, and sharing volleyball with so many people (your university, your community, and beyond).

Toronto's cricket story exists because there was no better way to plot out and explain immigration, generational handover, and unique ideas in a city with such an embedded history within Western colonization. Cricket may not be the first game one thinks about as a sport of choice, but it is a sport that, for some, is the centre of their world, and that deserved deep exploration on my part. Janelle Joseph, an academic I deeply respect, was pivotal to begin telling this story, and I thank her deeply for her contributions to this project. To Adam Vaughan, who has a litany of stories banked away about every subject under the sun, gave his time to this project, and I thank him for sharing his story. I would hope this city is filled with people like Adam – someone who loves to engage with others and is passionate about sports – even if the politics don't match up exactly. To Lauren Wolman and Lisa Grogan-Green, thank you for sharing the story of Michael Hough, Go Green Youth Centre, and what the future has in store for your unique project. I hope Go Green becomes a shining example of how communities can make better sports happen in their cities.

Ajahn Suchart Yodkerepauprai is such a magnetic, passionate person – and Muay Thai has given the city the gift of a sport with a deep cultural tie to another part of the world. That's what our city is – a place like the world and everyone in it. Thank you, Ajahn, for sharing your story. Muay Thai's trajectory will continue to shoot for the stars.

The Toronto Wolfpack project is a story without a conclusion so far. The club's time in Liberty Village should be a lesson that Big Sports adopts, but I hope there will be a sustainable sports ecosystem that supports the rugby community on a broad scale – on the field, but also in the community. Thanks to Jon Pallett, Bob Hunter, and Erik Grosman for bridging me over and helping me write this story.

I hope everyone takes the final chapters of this book as a call to action. We have to organize to move the needle and create the conditions for rapid change – to improve our health, gain autonomy in the public sphere, and make community sports an essential part of our civic growth. Arriving to these ideas came from speaking with futurists like Scott Smith and Madeline Ashby, who engaged me in one of the most refreshing conversations about the future I've ever had. Both were big inspirations and provided great insights that I could contextualize for this audience. Thank you both for helping me to finish this book. Thank you to Kristina Leis for sharing her story. Equally, thank you to Jon Solomon and the Aspen Institute for sharing your ongoing work through the Sports & Society Program. Their work tells me that our sports conversation is a broad one that needs to be had in every city and town. Our future – our children, spaces, and places – should always be our concern.

And with that, I hope your future, fair reader, is bright. Thank you, again, for reading this book.

BIBLIOGRAPHY

Books

Gairey, Harry. *A Black Man's Toronto 1914–1980: The Reminiscences of Harry Gairey*. University of Michigan Press, 1981.

Joseph, Janelle. *Sport in the Black Atlantic: Cricket, Canada and the Caribbean diaspora*. Manchester University Press, 2017.

Nakamura, Yuka. *Playing Out of Bounds: 'Belonging' and the North American Chinese Invitational Volleyball Tournament*. University of Toronto Press, 2019.

Subban, Karl and Scott Colby. *How We Did It: The Subban Plan for Success in Hockey, School and Life*. Random House Canada, 2017.

Szto, Courtney. *Changing on the Fly: Hockey through the Voices of South Asian Canadians*. Rutgers University Press, 2021.

Articles

Abdel-Shehid, Gamal. 'Toronto's multicultural Raptors: Teamwork and individualism,' *The Conversation Canada*, June 3, 2019, https://theconversation.com/torontos-multicultural-raptors-teamwork-and-individualism-118141.

Adlakha, Abhya. 'UTSC hosts, wins its first women's tri-series cricket tournament,' *The Varsity*, March 17, 2018, https://thevarsity.ca/2018/03/17/utsc-hosts-wins-its-first-womens-tri-series-cricket-tournament.

Ahmed, Shireen. 'UTSC, Ryerson and Laurier compete in groundbreaking tournament for women in cricket,' *University Affairs*, July 30, 2018, https://www.universityaffairs.ca/news/news-article/utsc-ryerson-and-laurier-compete-in-groundbreaking-tournament-for-women-in-cricket.

Aliu, Akim. 'Hockey Is Not for Everyone,' *The Players' Tribune*, May 19, 2020, https://www.theplayerstribune.com/articles/hockey-is-not-for-everyone-akim-aliu-nhl.

Allen, Kate, Jennifer Yang, Rachel Mendleson, and Andrew Bailey. 'Lockdown worked for the rich, but not for the poor. The untold story of how COVID-19 spread across Toronto, in 7 graphics.' *Toronto Star*, August 2, 2020, https://www.thestar.com/news/gta/2020/08/02/lockdown-worked-for-the-rich-but-not-for-the-poor-the-untold-story-of-how-covid-19-spread-across-toronto-in-7-graphics.html.

Allick, Chantaie. 'Bank flies in stars to help grow cricket in Canada,' *Globe and Mail*, June 26, 2011, https://www.theglobeandmail.com/news/toronto/bank-flies-in-stars-to-help-grow-cricket-in-canada/article591047.

Armstrong, Laura. 'Women's participation in sports is declining, according to Canadian Women and Sport survey,' *Toronto Star*, June 11, 2020, https://www.thestar.com/sports/2020/06/11/womens-participation-in-sports-is-declining-according-to-canadian-women-and-sport-survey.html.

Bascaramurty, Dakshana. 'How class and race are playing into COVID-19 restrictions and access to leisure,' *Globe and Mail*, June 12, 2020, https://www.theglobeandmail.com/canada/article-how-class-and-race-are-playing-into-covid-19-restrictions-and-access.

BET Staff 'Trey Songz Remembers Struggling Years With Drake,' Black Entertainment Television, October 25 2010, https://www.bet.com/news/music/2010/10/25/treysongzremembersstrugglemusicnews102510.html.

Bradburn, Jamie. 'Icy Discrimination,' *Jamie Bradburn's Tales of Toronto*, June 6, 2020, https://jamiebradburnwriting.wordpress.com/2020/06/06/icy-discrimination.

Brampton Guardian staff. 'City of Brampton begins renovation of Century Gardens Recreation Centre,' *Brampton Guardian*, May 1, 2007, https://www.bramptonguardian.com/news-story/3088811-city-of-brampton-begins-renovation-of-century-gardens-recreation-centre.

Buckner, Diane. 'Bike lanes installed on urgent basis across Canada during COVID-19 pandemic,' CBC News, June 7, 2020, https://www.cbc.ca/news/business/bike-lanes-covid-pandemic-canada-1.5598164.

Campbell, Morgan. 'Simon Marcus seeks GLORY in kickboxing title bout,' *Toronto Star*, May 7, 2015, https://www.thestar.com/sports/2015/05/07/simon-marcus-seeks-glory-in-kickboxing-title-bout.html.

canadianimmigrant.ca staff. 'Superfan, super Canadian,' *Canadian Immigrant* magazine, accessed January 2021, https://canadianimmigrant.ca/canadas-top-25-immigrants/canadas-top-25-immigrants-2018/nav-bhatia.

Canadian Press staff. 'Ontario to approve mixed martial arts events,' Canadian Press, care of CBC, August 14, 2010, https://www.cbc.ca/sports/ontario-to-approve-mixed-martial-arts-events-1.913168.

—. 'Super League votes unanimously to replace Toronto Wolfpack,' Canadian Press via CBC Sports, November 3, 2020, https://www.cbc.ca/sports/rugby/super-league-vote-toronto-wolfpack-replacement-1.5788031.

—. 'House of Commons passes law that takes MMA out of legal limbo,' Canadian Press via *Globe and Mail*, June 5, 2013, https://www.theglobeandmail.com/sports/more-sports/house-of-commons-passes-law-that-takes-mma-out-of-legal-limbo/article12363369.

Carson, Dan. 'Drake Finalizes Endorsement Deal with Jordan Brand, Previews New Shoe Line,' *Bleacher Report*, accessed October 2020, https://bleacherreport.com/articles/1875777-drake-finalizes-endorsement-deal-with-jordan-brand-previews-new-shoe-line.

CBC Radio. 'Confront racism when you see it in hockey, says Karl Subban,' Canadian Broadcasting Corporation, November 28, 2019, https://www.cbc.ca/radio/thecurrent/the-current-for-nov-28-2019-1.5376493/confront-racism-when-you-see-it-in-hockey-says-karl-subban-1.5376522.

Chow, Aaron. 'Kickboxing, Muay Thai, and Sambo Receive Full Olympic Recognition,' hypebeast.com, July 21, 2021, https://hypebeast.com/2021/7/kickboxing-muay-thai-and-sambo-receive-full-olympic-recognition-news crownscoutgirls.com. "Sami Hill Signs LOI With Virginia Tech," CROWN Scout Girls Basketball, November 20, 2012, https://www.crownscoutgirls.com/sami-hill-signs-with-virginia-tech.

Daily Hive Toronto staff. 'Kensington Market Pedestrian Sundays are back for the summer' Daily Hive Toronto, May 16, 2019, https://dailyhive.com/toronto/kensington-market-pedestrian-sundays-return-summer-2019.

Davidson, Neil. 'Toronto Wolfpack doomed to transatlantic failure thanks to rotten foundation,' Canadian Press via Toronto Star, November 2, 2020, https://www.thestar.com/sports/2020/11/02/toronto-wolfpack-fail-to-win-reinstatement-to-englands-top-tier-of-rugby-league.html.

Domise, Andray and Matthew Amha. 'Black hockey players on loving a sport that doesn't love them back,' Macleans, September 9, 2020, https://www.macleans.ca/sports/black-hockey-players-on-loving-a-sport-that-doesnt-love-them-back.

Donnelly, Peter, Simon Darnell and Bruce Kidd with Priyansh, Marc Lizoain and Mathew Blundell. 'The Implications of COVID-19 for Community Sport and Sport for Development,' University of Toronto, Faculty of Kinesiology and Physical Education, Centre for Sport Policy Studies, August 4, 2020, https://thecommonwealth.org/sites/default/files/inline/D17145_Sport_Covid_Series_PaperOne_V5.pdf.

Durnan, Matt. 'Subban family has special connection to Sudbury,' Sudbury.com, February 15, 2018, https://www.sudbury.com/local-news/subban-family-has-special-connection-to-sudbury-773425.

Douglas, William. 'P.K. Subban's dad talks hockey, life and catfish on new Color of Hockey podcast,' The Color of Hockey blog, October 3, 2017, https://colorofhockey.com/2017/10/03/p-k-subbans-dad-talks-hockey-life-and-catfish-on-new-color-of-hockey-podcast.

'Family Influence: The 2020 Participaction Report Card on Physical Activity for Children and Youth,' ParticipACTION, last accessed October 2020, https://www.participaction.com/en-ca/resources/children-and-youth-report-card.

Fitz-Gerald, Sean. 'Planets to Phantoms, Toros to Tornados: 10 Toronto teams you may have forgotten,' The Athletic, April 25, 2020, https://theathletic.com/1767176/2020/04/25/planets-to-phantoms-toros-to-tornados-10-toronto-teams-you-may-have-forgotten.

Grange, Michael. 'Great Canadian hoops legacies getting carried forward by Alexander, Hill,' Sportsnet, July 16, 2021. https://www.sportsnet.ca/olympics/article/great-canadian-hoops-legacies-getting-carried-forward-alexander-hill.

Gurney, Matt. 'End of an ice age, Part 2: How youth hockey became so expensive – and such a drag,' TVO, January 8, 2020, https://www.tvo.org/article/end-of-an-ice-age-part-2-how-youth-hockey-became-so-expensive-and-such-a-drag.

Hébert, Paul. 'Immigration Policy, the West Indies, and Canadian Black Activism in the 1960s,' African American Intellectual History Society, August 27, 2016, https://www.aaihs.org/immigration-policy-the-west-indies-and-canadian-black-activism-in-the-1960s.

'Hockey for Humanity – The Khalsa Cup,' Hockey 4 Humanity, care of Facebook, last updated Mar. 20, 2020, https://www.facebook.com/Hockey4Humanity.

Hussein, Nahabat. 'History: Plaque planned for track star Sam Richardson (May 2019),' *Annex Gleaner*, May 28, 2019. https://gleanernews.ca/index.php/2019/05/28/history-plaque-planned-for-track-star-sam-richardson-may-2019.

Jeffries, Doug. 'Queen's University roundtable says racism in hockey can no longer be tolerated,' *Global News*, April 9, 2019, https://globalnews.ca/news/5118859/queens-university-racism-in-hockey-roundtable.

Klores, Dan. 'Basketball has changed the world, and it can do even more,' *The Undefeated*, February 25, 2019, https://theundefeated.com/features/basketball-has-changed-the-world-and-it-can-do-even-more.

King, Perry. 'Shootings shock community: Police say recent violence mostly targeted,' *Annex Gleaner*, November 23, 2010, https://gleanernews.ca/index.php/2010/11/23/shootings-shock-community-police-say-recent-violence-mostly-targeted.

—. 'Central Tech's hoop dream come true,' *Globe and Mail*, February 3, 2017, https://www.theglobeandmail.com/news/toronto/central-tech-basketball-program-breaks-down-stigma-buildshope/article33896285.

—. 'Eastern Commerce, perennial high school basketball powerhouse, nears end,' *Toronto Star*, February 22, 2015, https://www.thestar.com/sports/basketball/2015/02/22/eastern-commerce-perennial-high-school-basketball-powerhouse-nears-end.html.

—. 'Cricket keep-up: changing demographics mean adapting facilities to reflect new needs,' *Spacing Magazine*, May 23, 2019, http://spacing.ca/toronto/2019/05/23/cricket-keep-up-changing-demographics-mean-adapting-facilities-to-reflect-new-needs.

Liang, Ursula. '9-Man – a streetball battle in the heart of Chinatown,' Kickstarter projects, October 31, 2014, https://www.kickstarter.com/projects/ursula/9-man-a-streetball-battle-in-the-heart-of-chinatow/description.

Loriggio, Paola. '"At home" in Little Tibet,' *Toronto Star*, May 15, 2008, https://www.thestar.com/news/gta/2008/05/15/at_home_in_little_tibet.html.

Lorinc, John. 'Power plays,' *Globe and Mail*, June 4, 2005, https://www.theglobeandmail.com/news/national/power-plays/article18228757.

Milley, Danielle. 'Cricket star Sunil Joshi visits Thorncliffe Park,' Toronto.com, June 24, 2011, https://www.toronto.com/community-story/65750-cricket-star-sunil-joshi-visits-thorncliffe-park.

Mitchell, Bob. 'Is big-time cricket headed to Toronto?' *Toronto Star*, April 10, 2013, https://www.thestar.com/sports/amateur/2013/04/10/is_bigtime_cricket_headed_to_toronto.html.

Norman, Mark, Peter Donnelly and Bruce Kidd. 'Gender inequality in Canadian interuniversity sport: participation opportunities and leadership positions from 2010-11 to 2016-17,' *International Journal of Sport Policy and Politics*, October 1, 2020, https://www.tandfonline.com/doi/abs/10.1080/19406940.2020.1834433?journalCode=risp20&.

North American Chinese Invitational Volleyball Tournament (NACIVT) Organizers, 'Brief History of 9-Man Volleyball,' bostonese.com online journal, accessed June 2021, https://bostonese.com/2015/03/brief-history-of-9-man-volleyball.

OurWindsor.ca staff. 'NBL Playoffs: Windsor Express take on Mississauga Power in quarter-finals,' OurWindsor.ca, March 3, 2014, https://www.ourwindsor.ca/community-story/4394632-nbl-playoffs-windsor-express-take-on-mississauga-power-in-quarter-finals.

Pagliaro, Jennifer. 'Family mourns 15-year-old teen Tyson Bailey fatally shot in Regent Park as police detail new evidence,' *Toronto Star*, January 28, 2013, https://www.thestar.com/news/crime/2013/01/28/family_mourns_15yearold_teen_tyson_bailey_fatally_shot_in_regent_park_as_police_detail_new_evidence.html.

Press Association. 'Toronto owner David Argyle stands down from roles after racism row,' *Guardian UK Sport.* June 8, 2019, https://www.theguardian.com/sport/2019/jun/07/rugby-football-league-investigate-toronto-owner-david-argyle-racial-abuse-swinton-jose-kenga.

Ryan, Megan. 'NHL bolsters its diversity efforts, though change is slow,' *Minnesota Star Tribune*, March 17, 2019, https://www.startribune.com/nhl-bolsters-its-diversity-efforts-though-change-is-slow/507254002.

Seravalli, Frank. 'Aliu speaks publicly on allegations against Peters,' *TSN Sports*, November 26, 2019, https://www.tsn.ca/akim-aliu-speaks-publicly-on-allegations-against-calgary-flames-head-coach-bill-peters-1.1403974.

Smith, Ainsley. 'Toronto Still Has Far More Cranes Up Than Any City in North America,' *Toronto Storeys*, April 9, 2020, https://storeys.com/toronto-most-cranes-north-america.

Town Crier staff. 'Eastern focuses on qualifying for OFSAA,' *Town Crier* (now called Streeter.ca), November 15, 2011, https://streeter.ca/toronto/news/sports/eastern-focuses-on-qualifying-for-ofsaa.

Tracy, Jeff. 'Exclusive: The impact of sports on LGBTQ youth,' *Axios*, September 3, 2020, https://www.axios.com/youth-sports-lgbtq-transgender-athletes-67c8e7b7-7e49-414b-a9e0-fdd910fcc947.html.

Weisfeld, Oren. 'Beloved coach Kareem Griffin has dedicated his life to growing women's basketball in Canada. Meet the game changer,' *Toronto Star*, May 2, 2021, https://www.thestar.com/life/together/people/2021/05/02/beloved-coachkareem-griffin-has-dedicated-his-life-to-growing-womens-basketball-in-canada-meet-the-game-changer.html.

Williams, Nadine. 'West Indian Domestic Scheme (1955–1967),' Parks Canada and the Historic Sites and Monuments Board of Canada, last updated July 31, 2020, https://www.canada.ca/en/parks-canada/news/2020/07/west-indian-domestic-scheme-19551967.html.

Woods, Dave. 'Toronto Wolfpack: New owner Carlo LiVolsi will underwrite losses if club readmitted to Super League,' *BBC Sport*, October 31, 2020, https://www.bbc.com/sport/rugby-league/54761414.

Reports

'75th NACIVT in Toronto final results!' NACIVT staff, last modified September 4, 2019, https://nacivtcom.wordpress.com/2019/09/04/75th-nacivt-in-toronto-final-results.

'2013–14 Men's Basketball Roster,' *University of Toronto Varsity Blues*, last modified August 8, 2018, https://varsityblues.ca/sports/mens-basketball/roster/alex-hill/6757.

'2016,' Toronto Short Film Festival, last modified March 18, 2016, http://www.torontoshort.com/2016-2.

'2020–21 Men's Basketball Training Squad,' *University of Toronto Varsity Blues*, accessed January 2020, https://varsityblues.ca/sports/mens-basketball/roster/evan-shadkami/12586.

'About CONNEX,' Toronto Connex, accessed June 2020, https://connexvb.wordpress.com/about.

'Ajahn Suchart Yodkerepauprai,' Siam No. 1 House of Muay Thai, last accessed June 2021, https://www.siamno1.com/ajahn-suchart.

'Apna Hockey,' Apna Sports International, accessed January 2020, https://apnasportsinternational.com.

'The BCCA – Did you know,' Black Canadian Coaches Association, last accessed June 2020, https://thebcca.com/did-you-know.

'BMO Field delivers $900,000 to City of Toronto, MLSE,' City of Toronto, last updated March 7, 2008, http://wx.toronto.ca/inter/it/newsrel.nsf/d7b6a6e7139d8f7785257aa700636487/e5c68d1b6129e3038525740500793be0.

'Census Profile, 2016 Census,' Statistics Canada, last modified August 9, 2019, https://www12.statcan.gc.ca/census-recensement/2016/dp-pd/prof/details/page.cfm?Lang=E&Geo1=FED&Code1=35081&Geo2=PR&Code2=35&SearchText=Parkdale--High%20Park&SearchType=Begins&SearchPR=01&B1=All&GeoLevel=PR&GeoCode=35081&TABID=1&type=0.

'CIMA Mayor's Trophy,' The Chartered Institute of Management Accountants, last updated May 2020, https://www.cimaglobal.com/Our-locations/Canada/CIMA-Branding-and-Community-Initiatives/CIMA-Mayors-Trophy.

'Eugene Arcand,' Wîcihitowin Indigenous Engagement Conference, accessed January 2021, https://wicihitowin.ca/speaker/eugene-arcand.

'Flemingdon Park: 2016 Neighbourhood Profile,' City of Toronto, published February 2018, https://www.toronto.ca/ext/sdfa/Neighbourhood%20Profiles/pdf/2016/pdf1/cpa44.pdf.

Galati, Luke. 'Bring Back Our Basketball Nets: Toronto District School Board,' change.org, last modified July 2019, https://www.change.org/p/bring-back-our-basketball-nets-toronto-district-school-board.

'The Global Liveability Index 2021,' *Economist Intelligence Unit*, https://www.eiu.com/n/campaigns/global-liveability-index-2021.

'Go Green Youth Centre,' University of Toronto School of Cities, last accessed June 2021, https://www.schoolofcities.utoronto.ca/GoGreenYouthCentre.

'GTHL Measures to Examine Discrimination in Minor Hockey,' Greater Toronto Hockey League, last updated June 12, 2020, https://www.gthlcanada.com/article/gthl-measures-to-examine-discrimination-in-minor-hockey.

'Home,' Canletes Basketball, last accessed January 2021, https://canletes.ca.

'Introducing the Vanguard,' Vanguard Toronto, last accessed January 2021, http://www.vanguardtoronto.com/#about.

'Kapapamahchakwew – Wandering Spirit School,' Toronto District School Board, accessed January 2021, https://www.tdsb.on.ca/Community/Indigenous-Education/Schools/Kapapamahchakwew-Wandering-Spirit-School.

'Masaryk-Cowan Community Recreation Centre,' Ontario Heritage Trust, accessed October 2018, https://www.heritagetrust.on.ca/en/pages/our-stories/exhibits/snapshots-of-ontarios-sport-heritage/connection-between-community-geography-and-sport/masaryk-cowan-community-recreation-centre.

'Neighbourhood Improvement Area Profiles,' City of Toronto, last accessed October 2020, https://www.toronto.ca/city-government/data-research-maps/neighbourhoods-communities/nia-profiles.

'OFSAA Past Champions Boys' Basketball,' Ontario Federation of Student Athlete Associations, last modified March 4, 2016, https://web.archive.org/web/20160304133318/http://www.ofsaa.on.ca/sites/default/files/Basketball%20-%20Boys%27%20%20Past%20Champions.pdf.

'Ontario Ready For Mixed Martial Arts,' Ontario Newsroom, last updated December 6, 2010, https://news.ontario.ca/en/release/15505/ontario-ready-for-mixed-martial-arts.

'Outdoor basketball court rentals – use of courts,' City of Toronto, last modified July 2019, https://www.toronto.ca/311/knowledgebase/kb/docs/articles/parks,-forestry-and-recreation/community-recreation/outdoor-basketball-court-rentals-use-of-courts.html.

'Project Play Summit,' Aspen Institute, last updated October 17, 2018, https://www.aspenprojectplay.org/summit/2018.

'Remembering Kobe Bryant,' Aspen Institute, last updated February 2020, https://www.aspenprojectplay.org/remembering-kobe#:~:text=KOBE%20AT%20THE%202018%20PROJECT,youth%2C%20sports%2C%20and%20health.

'Shifting Demographics and Hockey's Future,' National Hockey League, last accessed April 2020, https://nhl.bamcontent.com/images/assets/binary/300993502/binary-file/file.pdf.

'Spotlight On: The Central Tech Trio,' OSBA Communications, last modified February 28, 2020, https://www.ontariosba.ca/news_article/show/1091186.

'Susan Fennell,' Toronto Star, last accessed December 2020, https://www.thestar.com/news/gta/susanfennell.html.

'Tyson Bailey Fund,' Toronto Foundation, accessed January 2020, https://torontofoundation.ca/tyson_bailey_fund.

'Welcome to GTActivity,' GTActivity.ca research project, last updated July 2021, https://gtactivity.ca.

'Yonge St. bike lane would prove hugely popular,' David Suzuki Foundation, published October 5, 2020, https://davidsuzuki.org/expert-article/yonge-st-bike-lane-would-prove-hugely-popular.

Multimedia

'Eastern Commerce battles Oakwood for the Sr Boys AAAA City basketball title,' Toronto District School Board, last updated October 15, 2012, https://youtu.be/u6dcI9y-53w.

Nabag, Ebti. *At Home, In the Game,* care of Lay-Up Basketball, last modified October 22, 2020, https://www.layup.ca/ahitg.

'Skinny C's hoop dreams' *CBC Evening News,* broadcast date September 22, 1995, https://www.cbc.ca/archives/entry/skinny-cs-hoop-dreams.

'Trey Songz & Drake "Special Artist,"' Black Entertainment Television, last modified September 16, 2010, https://www.bet.com/video/106andpark/106guestrewind/trey-songz-drake-09-16-10-229805.html.

Perry King is an author, freelance journalist, communications strategist, and proud South Parkdale–raised Torontonian. With a literary focus on sports, education, and urbanism, Perry has bylines in *Spacing Magazine*, the *Toronto Star*, *Globe and Mail*, BBC, and a long list of independent newspapers and magazines.

Typeset in Albertina and Knockout.

Printed at the Coach House on bpNichol Lane in Toronto, Ontario, on Lynx Cream paper, which was manufactured in Saint-Jérôme, Quebec. This book was printed with vegetable-based ink on a 1973 Heidelberg KORD offset litho press. Its pages were folded on a Baumfolder, gathered by hand, bound on a Sulby Auto-Minabinda, and trimmed on a Polar single-knife cutter.

Coach House is on the traditional territory of many nations, including the Mississaugas of the Credit, the Anishnabeg, the Chippewa, the Haudenosaunee, and the Wendat peoples, and is now home to many diverse First Nations, Inuit, and Métis peoples. We acknowledge that Toronto is covered by Treaty 13 with the Mississaugas of the Credit. We are grateful to live and work on this land.

Edited by John Lorinc
Cover design by Michel Vrana
Interior design by Crystal Sikma
Author photo by Jalani Morgan

Coach House Books
80 bpNichol Lane
Toronto ON M5S 3J4
Canada

416 979 2217
800 367 6360

mail@chbooks.com
www.chbooks.com